Praise for *Rise Sister Rise*

'*Rise Sister Rise* is an incantation, an initiation, an invocation for you to remember the truth of who you are. Always, and in all circumstances, and especially right now. It's a potent mix of divine feminine history, spiritual memoir, incandescent poetry, and powerful mantras which will inspire you to unbind the magic within you. And it illuminates the sacred chant that's always resounding within the soul, both for ourself and for every woman we encounter: Rise Sister Rise!'

MEGGAN WATTERSON, AUTHOR OF *REVEAL*, *HOW TO LOVE YOURSELF*, AND *THE SUTRAS OF UNSPEAKABLE JOY*

'Rebecca is a ray of light, a refreshing soul. Her gift is evident. She is a role model for women, guiding us to embrace our power and awaken our authentic selves.'

LEANN RIMES, SINGER-SONGWRITER AND GRAMMY AWARD-WINNING ARTIST

'Rebecca Campbell is a grounded devotional spiritual teacher and messenger here to awaken and call in a new age. Her book *Rise Sister Rise* is a call to arms for women to remember their intuitive nature, unleash their potent power, and lead from the feminine.'

SONIA CHOQUETTE, *NEW YORK TIMES* BESTSELLING AUTHOR OF *TRUST YOUR VIBES*

'Rebecca Campbell is a modern-day High Priestess led by the Divine. I've never in my life met anyone who shines like she does. She has cultivated a sacred sisterhood where she holds the space for women to step into their ancient Goddess power now.'

KYLE GRAY, AUTHOR OF *WINGS OF FORGIVENESS* AND *RAISE YOUR VIBRATION*

'Rebecca and everything she shares is poetic, light-laden, and soul fuelled. She's a beacon and a heart-led guide for all who know that it is our time to rise.'

LISA LISTER, AUTHOR OF *LOVE YOUR LADY LANDSCAPE*

'*Rise Sister Rise* is a perfectly timed divine love letter written straight from Rebecca's deep, wide heart and delivered to today's female mystics through her kind, truthful and authentic voice. It is my honor to tread this path with Rebecca as my friend, sister and co-mystic, and I'm so happy for you that you hold this jewel in your hands right now. Take a breath, make yourself a cup of tea, and dive in to these words and the space they will create in your heart.'

HOLLIE HOLDEN, WRITER OF *NOTES ON LIVING AND LOVING*

D0068535

'I'm a super-fan of Rebecca Campbell... Rebecca guides her reader to step into their authentic power so that they can live and lead at their highest potential.'

'In my view Rebecca Campbell is the new era of leading-edge authors who empower women, and she will be recalled in a league with greats such as Erica Jong and Maya Angelou. *Rise Sister Rise* will be a well-loved bible on our book shelves 100 years from now.'

'Each new generation needs a new inspirational voice, and Rebecca Campbell is that voice. I just love witnessing a new, young talent about to unleash a storm that will change the way we think about our personal empowerment and spirituality.'

'Rebecca Campbell is a powerhouse lovingly pushing us into the next paradigm of love and healing. She's a force of femininity calling forth the truth, the power, the light, and the voice of all women who come in contact with her. *Rise Sister Rise* is sure to light that inner fire to change themselves, and by that act the world, through the women who open its magic pages. Blessings to Rebecca for her light on the planet in this perilous time. Jai Ma.'

'Rebecca is a vibrant and authentic voice in the emerging self-empowerment landscape, and effortlessly marries the numinous call of the soul with real-life wisdom for women on the rise.'

RISE
SISTER
RISE

A GUIDE TO UNLEASHING THE
WISE, WILD WOMAN WITHIN

REBECCA CAMPBELL

HAY HOUSE

Carlsbad, California • New York City • London
Sydney •Johannesburg • Vancouver • New Delhi

Published and distributed in the United States by: Hay House, Inc.: www .hayhouse.com® • **Published and distributed in Australia by:** Hay House Australia Pty. Ltd.: www.hayhouse.com.au • **Published and distributed in the United Kingdom by:** Hay House UK, Ltd.: www.hayhouse.co.uk • **Published and distributed in the Republic of South Africa by:** Hay House SA (Pty), Ltd.: www.hayhouse.co.za • **Distributed in Canada by:** Raincoast Books: www .raincoast.com • P**ublished in India by:** Hay House Publishers India: www .hayhouse.co.in

Cover and interior design: Leanne Siu Anastasi

Library of Congress Control Number: 2016947340

Tradepaper ISBN: 978-1-4019-5189-4

10 9 8 7 6
1st edition, October 2016

Printed in the United States of America

TO MY MOTHER, JULIE,
THE STRONGEST WOMAN I KNOW

AND

TO ANGELA WOOD (1947–2016),
WHO INITIATED MY SPIRITUAL PATH.

△

CONTENTS

Part II – Birthing A New Age

Part III – Remembering Our Cyclic Nature

Part IV – Unbinding the Wise, Wild Woman

Part VI – Doing the Work

△

I WANT YOU TO KNOW

This is not a book about women rising over men. This is a book of remembering a time when every woman was seen as sacred. And the divine feminine returning and rising just as She should. We are being called to bring about a balance between the feminine and masculine energies. Within ourselves and in our world at large. Both are sacred and needed. In order for this to happen, the sacred feminine that has been dormant and at times suppressed, needs to continue to rise. And She is rising. Can you feel Her?

I am aware that many reading this book are women and thus, for ease, I will be addressing women (She, Her). However, I want to stress that the rising feminine is not something that exists only within women, but rather it is within all things and people. As I talk about the importance of sisterhood, I too see the importance of brotherhood, the sacred masculine and the men who are great protectors, supporters, and lovers of the divine feminine, and her work in the world. I trust that there is an amazing guy writing that book in unison.

Throughout this book, you'll find references to Mother Earth, She, Her, Life, Source, God, Goddess, Father, Mother, Great Mother, Father/ Mother God, Beloved and the Universe. This is my humble attempt to put a name to the great mysteries and indescribable forces of our world and beyond, which is truly an impossible feat. If these words don't resonate with you, please trade them for your own.

You'll also find much reference to 'patriarchy.' That word, like 'feminism,' is so loaded. When I mention patriarchy it is to refer to the past few millennia, when society was led by a powerful few in a very linear way. An era when the sacred nature, power, and wisdom of the feminine was forgotten, controlled, silenced, or caged. When our connection to Mother Earth was severed. It is important not to see 'patriarchy' as the other. As we are making the shift from one age into the next, we must recognize that we have grown up in these patriarchal times and thus it is less about damning man and more about freeing and unchaining ourselves together.

While we are beginning to come out of this patriarchal age (referred to by some as the Piscean Age), I don't believe that the solution is for matriarchal energies to take its place. Rather, this book is an invitation for the intuitive, compassionate, wise, powerful, sacred, protective, fierce feminine force that exists within each of us to rise, and for the sacred masculine to protect and support Her rising and sacred work so that the planet can swing back into balance. The very fact that you have this book in your hands is proof that it is already happening.

You can read these pages in one sitting, one chapter a day, or pick a page at random for your instant hit of guidance (like an oracle deck). I recommend reading with a pen and notebook handy to capture the soul whispers that come to you, as you turn the pages. At the end of many of the chapters you will find *Rise Sister Rise* inquiry prompts. Do not underestimate the power of answering them. You have an ancient wisdom within you that is waiting for you to remember, hear, and heed it. These *Rise Sister Rise* calls to action have been carefully designed to assist you in reclaiming your voice, unbinding your power, unlocking your wisdom, unleashing your true nature, and aligning yourselves with the sacred flow of all of Life. Give them the weight that they deserve, they are your roadmap for rising.

I honor you for showing up to do this work at this time in Her story. As we gather we open the gates of healing in the collective consciousness. May it be felt by all. I believe in you, us and all of this.

Rise Sister Rise.

Rebecca

△

IT'S HAPPENING

Rise Sister Rise is a call to action for what is awakening within so many of us. An ancient remembering, dormant for centuries, which is more than beginning to stir. A conscious effort to end the persecution that we have inherited from patriarchy and been inflicting on each other.

It's time to awaken a new era of sisterhood on the planet.

One in which we bring back the balance of the sacred feminine and sacred masculine. One where we reconnect with Mother Earth, Mother God, the rhythm of the Earth, and our own natural rhythms. One where we draw our worth from deep within rather than letting the world decide it for us. One where we lead from the intelligent intuitive heart, know who we are with conviction, and live our lives in complete alignment and service to that. One where we realize that the only way to heal the world around us is by first healing ourselves. One where we heal the trauma we have inflicted on ourselves and our fellow sisters. One where we heal the patriarchy around us, as well as the patriarchy that resides within. One where we raise each other up rather than cutting each other down.

Rise Sister Rise.

Δ

TOOLS FOR YOUR RISING

My vision for *Rise Sister Rise* has always been more than just these pages. Below are some ways you can deepen your experience and connect with other rising sisters.

www.RiseSisterRise.com

Get over to www.risesisterrise.com for meditations, journeys, and tools mentioned throughout the book.

#RiseSisterRise

Share the light while you read using #RiseSisterRise
(I'm @rebeccathoughts)

Rise Sister Rise Spotify Soundtrack

Listen to the Rise Sister Rise Playlist while you read at www.risesisterrise.com

Join the Sisterhood

Join the Rise Sister Rise Sisterhood to receive monthly meditations and membership access to the private Facebook circle filled with many rising sisters. Join at www.risesisterrise.com

Part I

MY STORY

A non-linear journey of remembering,
unbinding, unshackling, and rising

THE UNBINDING

My whole life I had this knowing that there was something at the depths of me that was longing to be uncovered, released, expressed, unbound, unleashed, and set free. A potent force and ancient memory destined to be given a voice. For decades it scared me and so I devoted much of my life to keeping it (She) contained. Controlled. Submerged. Hidden.

As the years progressed, I could feel Her bubbling beneath the surface of my consciously created life. Beckoning for me to give up control, to allow Her to speak, to let Her roam wild, ecstatic and free. It was in nature that I heard Her most.

I could feel the lifetimes devoted to keeping Her bound up, hidden, and silenced, dormant for centuries. Unpredictable, inconvenient, relentless, inevitable, and powerful. The returning and rising of She.

The following pages describe my journey of remembering, reclaiming my voice, unbinding my power, unleashing the sacred wisdom within, surrendering to the cyclic nature of Life, and being held by the Mother. Like all things feminine, it will not be linear. But in my experience, rising never is.

△

THE WISE WOMEN

From an early age I was acutely aware of a yearning for the passing-down of wisdom, and soon began collecting older 'wise women' as best friends. Hungry for what they could teach me, I longed for their stories of heartache and adventure, inhaling all that their experiences could teach me that my years had not.

First came Angela Wood, who lost her daughter suddenly at the tender age of 15, the same age I was when I met her. Then came Sheila Dickson, who lived two doors down from my parents, 22 years my senior. Many more followed. I would listen for hours to their stories of womanhood and motherhood; gratitude and surrender; parenthood and adulthood; great love and loss; life, birth, and death. Soaking in all that I could, knowing I was learning much more from them than I ever could at school or university. A willing student, I decided that I was putting myself through my own Masters of Life.

I felt so at home around these women. With them, there wasn't the same distrust, uneasiness, and competitiveness that I felt with some of my peers. With my wise women, I could share my deepest dreams and greatest fears. I was able to show my whole self without holding any of it back. To discover and unleash my truest nature without trying to fit into a box. It was in conversation with these women that my soul's voice had the courage to speak.

Riding the bus home, listening to my yellow Walkman, I watched the world go by, as I dreamt of bringing them all together one day. All of these amazing wise women who had guided me, circled together in one room.

My mum was amazing at accepting these seemingly odd relationships. A compassionate, stylish, driven, selfless, strong woman, she intuitively knew that these relationships were somehow important.

When Mum first dropped me off at Angela's house, she walked me to her door and, in a single glance, Angela knew that Mum was handing me over to her while silently but fiercely saying, 'I am trusting you to look after my daughter.'

Last year, when Mum was going through her treasure box, she pulled out some old letters she had kept (I would often write letters to her when I was angry or upset, allowing my words to express what my voice could not). One read:

> *I know you don't understand my relationship with Angela.*
> *I don't either.*
> *But we both need to trust it, because it is important.*
> *And in years to come we will understand why.*

Looking back on my life I see how important my relationship with Angela was in informing the work I do today.

Just as in ancient times, in the days of the 'red tent' (when a woman was raised by a community of women and made all the richer for it, *see also page 112*) when I look back at these women – and so many more who along with my own mother played such an important role in my growth – I am humbled that they were there to guide me, and most deeply that my mother was able to see the importance of that.

WORK BABY

Born almost a month early, I was seemingly impatient to get on with what I came here to do; the day of my birth also marked the first day of Mum's new company. An award-winning fashion designer, she worked out of the garage with me in a cot beside her. When she secured the first factory space, my cot followed.

Working in an age when a woman's earnings weren't taken into consideration by banks and maternity leave in the private sector was non-existent, Mum was one of many women who forged the way for the next generation. She was ahead of her time, as was Dad – a schoolteacher who supported her wholeheartedly. One of three boys, raised in a family where his mother did absolutely everything, Dad made considerable leaps and bounds when it came to cooking, cleaning, and looking after my brother and me.

A true feminist at heart, Mum was determined that she could juggle it all. Be an amazing mother, as well as a highly successful career woman while always putting everyone else's interests ahead of her own – as so many women do. When traveling interstate or overseas, she would stay up until the wee hours making organic baby food and expressing milk. When saying my prayers before bed, she would remind me that I could do anything I wanted to, as long as I worked hard enough. I know I chose her for that.

I remember always being so proud of her for being such a successful businesswoman and, like most daughters, modeled myself on her. I've always been a natural empath and when Mum dropped me off at school, I could feel how her success and amazing outfits triggered some of the other mums. And how their presence triggered guilt and longing in Mum that she could spend more time with my brother and me. A double Virgo, determined to deliver her best at all times, every birthday I'd have homemade honey joys and chocolate crackles for my entire class. The evenings leading up to my birthday, you would find her at the sewing machine and, come my birthday morn, she would present me with the most amazingly crafted birthday dress, with a matching miniature one for my Barbie, My Child or Cabbage Patch Kid.

Each year she took on making costumes for the dance eisteddfod. Costumes so sequin-clad and impressive that if nominated for a Tony, they would surely win. Her efforts to give 110 percent at all times were both breathtaking and exhausting.

When Mum was a teenager she got pregnant and was sent away to a Magdalene-style convent for six months to have the baby. Only a handful of people knew. When she spoke about deciding what to do, she said that she knew in giving up her baby, she was giving her the best chance. Kylie, my half-sister, came back into her life 21 years later when I was 11, after her adoptive parents helped her track down her birth mother.

When Kylie asked Mum to make her wedding dress, she slaved over it for months on end. Each night after a long day at work, you'd find her armed with needle, thread and two pairs of reading glasses stacked on her nose, so as to hand sew thousands of the most intricate encrusted beads to the bodice. Meticulously pouring herself into that dress, almost in an effort to make up for what the years, times, and fate had not allowed.

SHAKTI RISING

'Shakti is the energy of the consciousness,
The divine creative energy, which creates an entire cosmos.'
MUKTANANDA

My first experience of Kundalini Shakti rising was in 1994 when I was 13. One of my schoolteachers started hosting a lunchtime meditation class. Instantly drawn to it, I showed up.

Lying on the floor, the teacher led the meditation by inviting us to let our bodies relax. After allowing my body to melt away and my spirit to connect with the Earth and Universe, I felt a powerful ecstatic energy rising through my body from the base of my spine and out of my head. I had never experienced anything even remotely like it and it made me uncomfortable – like I was about to burst. I had thought meditation was meant to feel like lying on a fluffy, cloud-like bed. My legs shook and my body jolted, and it freaked me out.

That night after school I told Mum about it, saying. 'It made me funny inside, like a wave made of honey moving through me and an electric shock.'

Overnight my art projects and creative stories began to take an ancient and spiritual turn. I found myself searching for this indescribable thing, this knowing, this remembering, this deep yearning and connection to the hidden sacred meaning of life. A Catholic schoolgirl, I prayed to Mother Mary to help me work it out. My prayers led me to a spiritual bookshop near my home where I spent hours on end.

I lied about my age to get my first job to support my crystal habit. Earning $3.13 an hour, I couldn't afford much, so would just hang out there running my hands through the buckets of crystals and reading as much as I could without buying the books.

I remember pulling *You Can Heal Your Life* by Louise Hay off the shelf and in that moment I knew with conviction that I was here to create a body of work just like the authors that filled the bookshelf. I saw myself speaking on stage and sharing my thoughts, feelings, and visions with audiences around the world. The thought of it both scared and excited me.

I tried bringing some of my friends to the shop and sharing my awakening with them, but no one seemed to understand and they looked at me like I was crazy. It triggered a fear in me of being cast aside for my beliefs, so at this tender age I made the conscious decision to step into a spiritual closet and began living a double life. By day I was a normal teenager, by night I would inhale all that I could about the journey of the soul and ancient lands. I longed to share this part of my life with people my own age. Every now and then I would reveal this part of me to those few I deemed safe. That was where my wise women came in. With them I could express my thoughts, visions, and feelings freely.

△

IMRAMMA: BRITISH ISLES

*'Imramma: The crossing of the deep waters, the wonder
voyage, where we don't know where we are going, only
that we are on our way somewhere our soul needs to go.'*
LUCY CAVENDISH, LOST LANDS

When I finished high school I deferred starting university and took three
jobs to save up enough money to get me to the UK. I didn't know why I
was going, only that I must and had to do it on my own. After reassuring
my parents not to stress, I got on the plane and it wasn't until I landed
that I realized I had absolutely no idea what I was doing.

Setting down roots in Dublin, Ireland, I worked as a part-time nanny for
a distant relative and spent my spare time on a solo pilgrimage of the
sacred sites of Ireland, England, and Scotland.

At Newgrange my connection with the light was initiated. In the
Scottish Highlands I had my first physical spirit experiences evidenced in
my photographs. On the Isle of Skye I felt the presence of the mystical
veil between two worlds lift, and in London I discovered how it feels to
be truly anonymous. Journeying to different towns, cities, sacred sites,
stone circles, and cemeteries that nature had reclaimed, I couldn't shake
the feeling that I was retracing my steps. Collecting memories my soul
had planted. Some came as past-life visions, others as familiar knowings
or feelings – like recalling a dream just after you awaken.

I arrived back in Sydney with a photo album packed with Celtic crosses
from overgrown graveyards, megalithic stone circles and Celtic triple
spirals – all symbols and patterns that seemed so familiar to my soul. I

knew with conviction that something significant had been ignited and that someday soon I would return.

Five years and four flights later, I landed back in London, with a university degree and my entire life on my back. I made my way to my new flat in Stockwell, working visa in hand and a heart full of hopes and fears, doubts and dreams filling my body and mind. Once again, I had no idea why I was here, only that I needed to be. Something about this land was beckoning me. It would take me several years to discover what.

△

MAKING IT IN A MAN'S WORLD

Getting my first job as a junior creative felt like the best day of my life at the time – like I was *finally* going somewhere and could begin to contribute my unique ideas to the world. While my spiritual life was of utmost importance, I had made the decision to go undercover as a Lightworker. I chose advertising because I could see how many ads bombarded us each day, and thought I could put good energy into these spaces rather than manipulation. Looking back I see how I was really just too scared to do the work that I do today. But also how this career was a brilliant training ground for the work that I do now.

The industry was exciting, extremely competitive, and exhausting, with deadline after deadline and no downtime in between. It was here that I learned to endure and strive. As the years went on, I forged a successful career by squashing my empathic nature and drawing on my masculine reserves to make it in a man's world. I remember consciously deciding to change my behavior and even the way that I dressed in order to be taken seriously as one of the guys.

I cringed when older male colleagues apologized for swearing 'in the presence of a lady,' and so joined in with my own language, in order to make a point of being more like them. I forced myself to work ridiculous hours (way longer than my male counterparts) in an effort to prove myself and not appear to be 'weak.' I pushed down my feminine power, sensitivities and innate intuitive wisdom, in order to climb the linear ladder. Ignoring my body's natural rhythms in favor of endurance.

Weekends were spent in recovery mode, desperately trying to refill my well in time to do it all over again come Monday morning. In a constant state of adrenal overload, I kept myself going during the day with bucketloads of black Americanos and in the evenings chased it all down with a fat glass of red. In my spare time I trained in the intuitive and healing arts and was blown away by how much it energized me and lit me up.

I didn't respect my monthly cycle, keeping myself propped up on a monthly diet of heavy-duty painkillers and trips to the disabled toilets where, some months, I would lie in the fetal position when the cramps got too much to bear. I was so invested in being the 'hard worker,' the 'dedicated soldier,' 'the endurance runner,' the 'good girl who never complained,' always finding a way to keep on pushing on. Of withstanding and shape-shifting my way through life.

I measured my input in a linear fashion, often the last one in the office, believing that effort equaled output. When people would ask me how I was, I would respond with something along the lines of 'super busy' or 'exhausted, as I've been working super long hours,' as if being in demand and stretched defined my worth. My ego felt important but my soul was completely parched.

I reached my long-term goal of becoming a Creative Director of a London advertising agency before 30. It felt like nothing. No one made me do any of this. I had chosen to do it, to fit into a system that did not fit my soul. Something needed to change.

Listening to Her whispers, two girlfriends and myself packed our bags for a sacred pilgrimage from Istanbul to Cairo through Turkey, Syria, Jordan, and Egypt. Backpacks checked in, we had no idea that our lives were about to change forever.

△

IMRAMMA: PETRA

It is dark. I can't see further than a few steps in front of me. I am walking through the desert in Jordan down a winding candlelit path. Every few minutes I pull my camera out to take a picture, in an effort to capture all of the emotion I am feeling. The flash lights up the rock formations above me, giving me a glimpse of ancient carvings. I look down at the screen on my camera to discover each picture is filled with an ocean of orbs. A heartening confirmation that I truly am in the most memorable place my human body has trodden. With every new step I am remembering. My soul is drinking it all in.

It was 2010 in the ancient city of Petra. After about 60 minutes, the path opens up and I enter a rose-colored rock carved out like a womb filled with a sea of tea lights. My eyes focus on the ruins of the ancient library before me and my soul feels like it has finally come home. I had visited this place so often in my dreams, without ever knowing it really existed. Every time I envisaged the Akashic Records* in my intuitive sessions or personal journeys, this is the place I went to in my mind's eye.

I returned the next day in the light to retrace my steps under a great blue sky. Remembering and praying in her cool caves, carved by the winds of time. With every breath, lifetimes spent on this land flooded my heart. Long-forgotten threads of the tapestry weaving together with each new moment. Old poems etched in my heart whispered to me, as my soul stretched the threads that joined the worlds. It felt as though

---

* The Akashic Records are the collection of mystical knowledge that is stored in the non-physical plane of existence – the æthers. *Akasha* is a Sanskrit word meaning 'sky,' 'space,' or 'æther.' Also referred to as The Book of Life, the Akashic Records are an account of all that has been, is and ever will be – past, present, and future.

I had been journeying to get here for lifetimes. And, as happens with sacred spaces that our soul knows more than our mind, something was activated in the ancient depths of me. A seed planted long ago, was finally ignited. Now, at last it was time.

△

IMRAMMA: WADI RUM

Lying there, in the dried-up, ancient ocean floor that was now a desert as vast as any, I could still hear the ocean whispering tales of changing times and forms. Under a canopy of the brightest stars my eyes had ever seen. Ear to the Earth, my heart shown what my soul had come here to remember – the sea of women who had trodden this path and all who will continue to come again. A sacred force of sisterhood, weaving their medicine and light in every corner of the Earth. Linked together by a luminous red thread woven from heart to heart. I closed my eyes and continued to remember and awaken as I drifted off to sleep.

△

THE CRUMBLING

Returning to London after my pilgrimage through the sacred sites, I knew that life couldn't continue, as it had before. I could feel the crumbling coming.

Having been in my spiritual closet for more than 15 years, I felt more trapped than ever. No matter how many teachers I trained with or qualifications I received, I still didn't feel ready to step into the work that my soul was calling me to do because of an indescribable fear that I would be persecuted for my beliefs.

The tighter I clung to the life I'd consciously created, the harder it got to hold it together. Before long my life began falling around me. Kali, the compassionate, dark mother appeared with her sword, severing any part of my life that was not in alignment with who I came here to be. My decade-long relationship ended, one of my best friends died suddenly, followed by another, and when I moved to a new apartment, I discovered that that was falling apart also.

It brought me to my knees. My ego finally begged for mercy and asked my soul to lead. I committed to answering the call for real and began the serious business of aligning my life to my soul. Like a striptease, revealing my true self to those around me. I committed to my spiritual practice and sharing Her whispers like an ancient warrior in training. I felt more scared and alive than ever.

△

SHAKTI RISING II

*'Once the Shakti is unfolded, the inner yoga
begins to take place spontaneously. That yoga
happens by itself; you don't have to do it.'*
MUKTANANDA

After two years of non-negotiable spiritual practice consisting of Light Sourcing (*see page 258*) and body shaking, one morning I woke up feeling extremely joyous and noticed that my whole body was convulsing of its own accord. It was like I was having some sort of epileptic fit, only it actually felt good, ecstatic even. I went to the doctor and had a whole lot of tests. I was in perfect health.

Some nights I would wake up to my whole body shaking and my teeth chattering at a crazy speed that I could not even try to re-create. I shared my experiences with one of my teachers and she informed me that they were the side effects of your Kundalini Shakti beginning to rise.

At work, I'd be sitting at my desk and out of nowhere one of my legs or my body would jolt and jerk on its own accord. On a couple of occasions in meetings, I caught my neck jolting and tried to restrain it, so as not to look like a crazy lady or as if I'd nodded off mid-sentence. Sometimes I would be overwhelmed by a surge of a kind of ecstatic sexual energy and feel my whole body getting physically hot. All this was the result of my Shakti serpent uncoiling and beginning to rise.

The Shakti would sometimes shoot from my head to my toes, like being charged up like a battery and cleared out in some way. Sometimes it felt warmer and fluid, like sweet nectar intertwining each of my chakras and cracking open my heart. It felt like the heavens and earth were connecting through my body.

I began having visions and dreams of past lives. Of times I had been persecuted for speaking out and trusting my innate wisdom and power – my past lifetimes as the healer, Priestess, the mystic, the poet, and the witch. The burning times when so many of us were silenced and killed for speaking out, for sharing our wisdom, and standing in our feminine power. For worshiping the seasons, understanding our natural ability to heal, sharing our medicine, and honoring the Earth.

It was as if these ancient memories had been locked away and the rising of the Shakti had released the lid to a carefully sealed vault. It was uncomfortable and liberating. Finally I understood why I was so scared to share my voice and step into my role as a spiritual writer, healer and teacher. How even though I knew with certainty that this is what I came here to do, still I wavered.

During these few months of my Shakti rising, I would shift in and out of periods of normality, from the trauma of processing past lives to complete euphoria. I began seeing sacred geometry and how everything was connected, like seeing the blueprint to all of life. I felt like Dorothy stepping into a new land where everything was all of a sudden in Technicolor.

I would look at a flower petal and understand how it was connected to the larger whole. I would sit in the bath and go into the intricacies of a single bubble, almost like I was able to morph into it myself. Sometimes an hour would pass and it felt like a minute. Other times a minute would pass and it felt like an hour. Time got stretchy.

I would pass a tree and feel it whisper directly into my heart. Lying on the Earth, I could feel Her pulse and received the energy that surged beneath charging me up. I felt one with the entire planet – my energy connected to the Shakti of the entire Universe, like one big river or ocean of Life. I didn't own the Shakti, rather I was simply allowing it to flow through me. I felt more alive than ever.

After a few months the teeth chattering and spontaneous jolting started to ease. But I was forever changed. A force within me had remembered and awakened, and now awakened it wasn't going to sleep. It would be a while before I could find the words to describe this period of my life.

I vowed to answer the calls of my soul and the Universe, no matter how much sense it made or how scary it was. I began sharing my writing and teaching groups. On my morning walks I would hear whispers from Mother Earth, just as I did when I was a young girl. These whispers turned into my first book *Light Is the New Black*. I was in flow with She and She was in flow with me.

A year later when I met my now husband Craig, I experienced my third Shakti rising, spurred on in the coming together of the sacred masculine and feminine energies. But that's a story for another time (and perhaps another book).

IMRAMMA: SANTA FE

The publishing date for my first book, *Light Is the New Black,* was rapidly approaching and my flight instincts were peaking. In three weeks I was to take the stage in front of 500-plus people at my first major speaking gig.

I find myself in Santa Fe, standing in front of my speaking coach, Gail Larsen, and four peers. I am there to face my fears around sharing my voice. While I had become comfortable sharing my writing, the thought of standing on a stage in front of so many people was making me nervous.

I had been teaching workshops for three years, but still after all this time, there was part of me that could not shake the irrational feeling that I was going to be killed for what I had to say. There was no rational reason for this fear, but still it was there.

From the moment I landed in Santa Fe I could feel a grapefruit-sized lump lodged in the center of my throat. No matter what I did, I could not swallow, soothe, or force it down. Encouraged by the black obsidian beneath my feet, I could feel that age-old pattern of holding back my voice about to erupt all over the place. Fighting to hold down the tears and entrap the citrus bulge, which now seemed to have developed razor-blade-like edges, I did my best to get through the morning by not speaking at all.

Just before we break for lunch I am instructed to stand in front of the group to do a 15-minute speech. Off the cuff. Without even 30 seconds to prep. Video camera on record. Eyes locked on me. Had I really chosen to be there of my own freewill?

I decide that if I had a superpower, teleportation would be it.

I am encouraged just to share what emotions are going through me at that moment. Through a shaking defensive voice, I state... that is what I am scared of.

I take a deep breath and soon discover that this feeling that I had been holding back was a surprising concoction of grief and rage. Through staccato sobs, I confess:

'I am so furious with God/dess right now, I cannot even begin... I mean seriously, why does the work I am here to do have to involve doing the very thing that scares me most?

'How can I possibly encourage other people to share their soul's voice, when I am so petrified to do it myself? Why is this my message? It's so unfair. I mean, why can't my message be about style or health or creativity or quite frankly anything but this?'

After what felt like an eternity, the sobbing made way for something else – a sound current foreign to my ears, yet familiar to my soul. She spoke with cadence, clarity, wisdom, and conviction.

And She had a lot to say.

△
FREEING MY VOICE

The moment I discovered chanting it felt like coming home. For the first few months of practicing regularly, I cried pretty much every day. Not tears of sadness, but the joyful tears of being reunited with myself (Self), of coming home. I was finally allowing the voice of my soul to sing. The chanting filled me up like sweet nectar, and, each time I sang, it was as if I was not doing the singing, rather, it was I who was being sung.

I bought myself a harmonium (a very clunky, unsexy Indian musical instrument that makes the most heart-bellowing sounds) and started playing it each day as part of my spiritual practice. One by one, women who were connected to chanting started entering my life. As they did, a little light went off inside me, as if to say, 'Bing, bing, bing, yes this, follow this.'

Following the golden thread being woven before me, I began working with my teacher and friend Nikki Slade in truly freeing my voice from the lifetimes of soul trauma that I'd discovered through my Shakti Awakening. Using the power of the vibration of my voice I was able to remember, embody, voice, and release it all. Lifetimes of unexpressed rage, grief, agony, sadness, loss, betrayal, guilt, and despair were finally set free through the power of my voice.

One by one, clients began coming to me with similar soul traumas from times of persecution – witches, healers, High Priestesses, midwives, teachers, medicine women, seers, Knights Templar, and diviners from times past. All with a knowing of the work they had returned here to do, with an unshakable fear of rising to it. Together we would journey and call those pieces back home. Renouncing vows of silence made in times where it was the only way to survive. Witnessing the pain and suffering that living in these times entailed. Being persecuted for sharing their truth, medicine, and gifts with the world. For working with the seasons and seeing all people as holy.

As more and more clients arrived at my door with the same symptoms, I started seeing a pattern. Many of us experienced a sense of urgency to rise up, come out of our spiritual closets, realign our lives, and do this work in around 2012 – the year that the Mayan calendar ended and a new age was called in, which I'll discuss in more detail later (*see page 49*).

It was as if during this time something shifted. In the ending of one age and the beginning of another the feminine vow of silence was lifted. Right on cue each of us beginning to come out of hiding, intuiting that it was finally safe to be fully seen and once again rise.

△

NO LONGER SUSTAINABLE

Light Is the New Black was finally out on the shelves and having been in a spiritual closet for so long, I felt like I had to give it my all in an effort to make up for lost time.

While I had written the book and created a whole new life for myself by surrendering to the mysterious flow of She, I had no idea how to integrate this new way of being into running my business. A career girl who learned to make it in a man's world, I reverted to the old patriarchal ways of enduring, pushing, and striving. Of being the hard worker, the dutiful soldier, the good girl. Using pressure not pleasure as my driving force. Putting my service to others above service to myself.

My client sessions were booking out three, four, five, six months in advance. I kept promising myself that I would tend to filling my inner well when things quieted down. But days turned into weeks, and weeks into months.

My time in nature was rationed to trips to the closest park, which didn't touch the edges of what my soul was truly yearning for. I even began approaching my daily devotional spiritual practice with a sense of duty. It was ever so subtle, but every decision I made took me further away from the rhythm of Me and thus She and Life.

Each time I took a step in the direction of my old ways of being I was resisting being held by the mysterious force that not only nourished me most but also was responsible for the effortless flow of all of Life. Acting from a place of pressure and endurance, I was resisting being held by the Mother and Life.

She/the Universe began sending me messages. Each time I sat down for a client session or an interview, the builders, working two doors down, would start drilling. Tuning in to the subtle energy of the soul is quite challenging with high-pitched machinery shrieking around you.

I knew that I was here to create a life's work, not a season. But at this rate it wouldn't be possible. There had to be a different way...

One Friday morning I woke up sobbing after having one those dreams that are just so real. In the dream I had a baby girl. Everyone was in awe because she never ever cried. But because she didn't cry, a whole week passed without her receiving any nourishment. Guilt-stricken for failing to look after her, I scooped her up and brought her to my breast, feeding and rocking her, mothering her and doing all I could to get her to receive. I looked down at this beautiful baby girl and as she looked so lovingly up at me I recognized her soul as my own. She then morphed into my mum's.

Feeling the deep sadness of this dream I didn't move for about an hour, doing all that I could to hold on to the importance of the message and also sending love to my mum.

When I got up I checked my phone and discovered a text from my dad to call home. Feeling the energy behind the text, I knew it was not good news.

Mum had breast cancer. Dad wasn't meant to be calling me because Mum didn't want anyone to know (her younger sister also had cancer and was scheduled for surgery to have her bladder removed), and didn't want anyone to worry. Dad suggested that I call Mum and say that I had a dream about her and wanted to check that she was OK. I told him about the dream and that I wouldn't have to lie.

Looking up the metaphysical meaning of breast cancer, I discover it is to do with a refusal to nourish yourself and the ability to receive – the meaning of my dream. Like the majority of women I know, my mum is a total giver, putting every other person's needs ahead of her own. I saw how I was doing the same thing with my work once again. Like the baby in my dream, and like so many other women, my mum and I had been denying ourselves the nourishment that we needed.

One Monday morning, just as the drilling started up for the week, I fell to my knees and prayed to the Mother to show me the way. And immediately got a response, 'Halve your work hours, double your devotion, and go to the Chalice Well Gardens in Glastonbury.'

Knowing guidance when I hear it, 15 minutes later my overflowing diary had been cleared, bus ticket booked, and the blue angel room reserved at my favorite guesthouse on Wellhouse Lane, on the outskirts of Glastonbury.*

The day before I left for Glastonbury, my friend Jayne introduced me to Madeline Giles who was visiting from the USA. The moment our eyes meet I know I've found a Magdalene sister.

Unable to find the words, Madeline and I end up just looking at each other while awkwardly smiling and laughing. When I tell her how disappointed I am that my upcoming trip to Glastonbury means we can't spend more time together in London, she reveals her purpose for being in the UK: To tour the sacred sites of Glastonbury with Kundalini teacher Guru Jagat.

We make plans to meet for afternoon tea.

I already feel like I am in another world.

---

* Glastonbury is a small town in Somerset in the UK. It is a sacred place where the veil between the worlds is extra thin. It is also where the Michael and Mary ley lines of the Earth meet. Likened to meridian points of the planet, many ancient sacred sites, stone circles, temples and churches around the world were built on these ley lines, in order to harness the powerful feminine energy of the Earth (Shakti) that runs beneath. Avalon is an ancient land between the worlds and Glastonbury is thought to be the location of one of its main communities.

Δ

RETURNING TO AVALON

Three days later I found myself lying, star-shaped, in a patch of daffodils in the Chalice Well Gardens. My inner well being replenished to the sound of the red springs bubbling eternal.

I allowed the full weight of my body to be held by the Earth, as it nourished me in ways that I hadn't been able to do for myself. My heart began to balance to the beat of She.

Surrendered in Her arms, my soul drank it all in. Supported by the Shakti running through the sacred ley lines beneath me. I could feel the feminine energy of the Earth beginning to spiral through me, like nectar replenishing the most undernourished of places, connecting each of my chakras.

Hour by hour my parched soul was quenched, my hardness softened, my brittleness made fertile, as pressure gave way to pleasure.

The next day, I began to hear Her whisper again, as I had before on my first visit to Glastonbury. I surrendered to the plan greater than me, picked up a pen and began writing the name and outline for this book. All the time, in awe at how much easier life is when I surrender to Her embrace.

In the margins I wrote down several sacred places in the UK that I felt called to visit for the book (and my own pleasure), including Merlin's Cave, Nectan's Glen, Avebury, and the crop circles in Wiltshire (which I had discovered was the home of some of my ancestors).

Lying there in the Chalice Well Gardens, I thought of Madeline and couldn't shake the feeling that perhaps I was meant to be on the same sacred trip that she had journeyed here for. I delegated the decision to the Universe by declaring, 'Alright, Universe, if I am meant to be on this trip, organize it for me and organize it quick.'

Back at the guesthouse, as I put on my favorite chanting music and got ready to take a bath, there was a knock. I opened the door to find a white-clad yogi called Ra Ma Kaur standing there, asking me if I was there for the sacred tour with Guru Jagat starting the next day.

With a disbelieving laugh I responded, 'I think I am,' and then relayed to her what I'd just delegated to the Universe. She then pulled out her phone to text the event organizer Shabadpreet, and 30 seconds later I was booked in.

The next day I joined a group of 30 turban-wearing yogis to begin chanting our way around the UK's sacred sites. My breath was taken away again, as I discovered that the tour was not just going to Glastonbury as I thought, but also to Cornwall to St Nectan's Glen, Merlin's Cave in Avebury and... wait for it... crop circles too!

My quick trip of rejuvenation was rapidly turning into an 11-day, life-changing magical adventure, as I kept extending my trip.

Whole days spent praying, chanting, and connecting with the wisdom of some of the planet's most sacred sites. Chanting as the sun rises over the Tor, lying on the St Michael and Mary ley lines, and sending my light to the corners of the Earth, meditating in the middle of sacred stones in Avebury, surrendering our creations to the Goddess at St Nectan's Glen (where myths suggest that the Knights Templar would go to be blessed by the High Priestesses before and after battle) and, most significantly, Merlin's Cave...

△

MERLIN'S CAVE

Walking into the cave my heart began to palpitate and my body was covered in chills. In an instant I knew my soul had been there before. As I made my way deeper into the dramatic rock-like retreat, I pulled out my phone to take a picture. As I did, I felt a flash of light fly in front of me and above my head. I looked at my phone and saw the shape center front in my photo. Moving further into the cave, I shared it with Madeline. To her disbelief she replied, 'Me too!' Comparing our phones we saw the exact same shape appearing like the outline of a man moving above us.

Looking at each other, something inside us knew that we had been brought together for this moment in time. Wearing knee-high rubber boots, we waded through the icy dark waters and over a sea of jagged rocks to the other side of the cave where the sky and ocean meet. With moody waves crashing at our feet it was impossible not to feel the power of the elements coming together in potent force. Climbing up to a flat rock sheltered above, we joined hands and began to meditate together.

Soon after closing my eyes, I had a vision of us in my mind's eye: part of a group of Priestess initiates at the end of our training. Before us was Merlin and another woman. Madeline, the other initiates, and I were overcome with a sense of fear and trepidation at the thought of going out into the world. We knew that after this day we would be leaving the protective bubble of our guides and sisters behind us to venture back out into the world at a time of much turmoil.

Merlin's energy was fierce and forceful as he spoke to us in a way that was both relevant then and today.

*It is time to go out into the world and share what you have
learned, what we have taught you, what you came here to
do. Now is not the time to cower, now is the time to rise.
Now is not the time to have your head in the clouds, now is
the time to claim your potency, ground your light and lead
with conviction. To do as you have been trained to. To do
the work that you were born to do. To lead, lead, lead.*

He then looked at me as if addressing me in current time and said:

*The burning times are over. The time of doing
this work alone or underground has come to an
end. You do not need to hide anymore.*

*This is the age that we have been working for. So pull
yourself together, stand tall, rise up and lead. All of the
lifetimes of training has been for now. You are held
by many. Call upon them and all that you have been
taught through the ages, for it has been for this exact
moment in time. Go forth and lead, lead, lead.*

And then all of a sudden, he was gone.

I opened my eyes to discover I was sobbing. Madeline squeezed my hand
and I found her in the same state. Relaying what had just happened to
each other, we discovered that we had had the same experience.

Leaving the cave Madeline and I shared our pictures with the rest of the
group, who had also been taking photos in the cave at the same time.
The figure of light only appeared in Madeline's and my photographs.

△

WHITE SPRINGS RITUAL

Craig and I were to be married in December in Australia, and leading up to the wedding I felt a deep yearning to honor the transition I was about to make, as I crossed the threshold into womanhood. My friend and commissioning editor Amy Kiberd asked me if I was planning to have a hen party in the UK before leaving and I confessed that I had been avoiding it but what I would really love is an intimate ritual. Amy suggested she organize it. I said, 'YES!'

A month later, Amy, Hollie Holden, Lisa Lister, and I all piled into Hollie's car and made our way to Glastonbury to hold a ritual the next day at the White Springs.

We arrived at an ancient guesthouse, where Joseph of Arimathea* is reputed to have been a regular, stopping over on his journeys to the Isle of Avalon.

Greeted by a strapping young man wearing very tight white jodhpurs, we all tried to hold back our teenage-girl laughter, as he escorted us (four grown women) to the family room we had opted for, because... sleepover!

We opened the door to discover a heavily floral clad room. Floral bedspreads, floral wallpaper, floral chairs, floral pillows, two floral single beds, and a floral canopy over the smallest double bed on Earth, where Amy and Lisa would end up sleeping that night.

---

* Legend suggests that Joseph of Arimathea was Mother Mary's uncle, thus Jesus' great uncle. Legend says that Joseph traveled to Britain with the young Jesus, and after the Crucifixion brought the Holy Grail to Glastonbury and established the first Christian church here.

Under the floral canopy slumber party style, Amy pulled out a gourmet array of snacks and champagne. The perfect start to what would become a regular 'Spiritual Sleepover Sisterhood' (The SSS), consisting of the spectacular combination of great food, conscious company, and ritual.

The next morning we sat together in circle. Adorned with handwritten wishes, blessings, and symbolic gifts, we passed a red egg (symbolizing my womb and ability as a woman to create both within and outside my body) around the circle, whispering wishes into it.

I was asked to share my intention for the ritual: To step into my power as a woman, unbind myself from those things that are no longer mine to carry, and break the chain so I could enter the marriage as a woman one-in-herself. Hollie, Lisa, and Amy listened deeply. I never felt so held and so heard.

A flower crown was placed upon my head and I was told what the ritual would entail. These incredible women would hold the space and highest intention for me to reclaim any lost pieces of my power and voice as a woman, as I moved between them and through each stage of womanhood. Amy, Hollie, and Lisa would each embody one of the archetypes of the Triple Goddess: Amy as the Maiden, Hollie as the Mother, Lisa as the Crone, and me as the Wise, Wild Woman who would be transitioning throughout.

Their ability and willingness to be in complete service to my unbinding and rising was deeply humbling and moving. Before we left, I burst into tears, in deep gratitude for them being so truly there. Even before the ritual had taken place, they had expanded my capacity to receive.

I confessed that I had been craving this kind of circle, this sisterhood, my whole life and that it would be my deepest honor to be able to do the same for each of them. They affirmed that they had been craving it too and were receiving it by being there – the power of women circling. Magic was already being woven.

Arriving at the White Springs, we were greeted by one of the keepers, who escorted us inside and locked the door behind us. With a bang of the door, I was reminded how haunting the acoustics can be in there. Surrounded by candlelight, we stepped into the dark womb-like cave at the belly of the Tor to the soundtrack of the springs thundering before and below us. It was freezing in there yet a light we could feel but not see warmed us. As we walked deeper into the springs, I was overcome with a feeling in the depths of my own womb. She had already started moving through me. I had no idea that I was about to have one of the most powerful experiences of my life, one that would set off a chain of events both for me and in my female line.

In the three corners of the White Springs are altars devoted to different parts of the feminine and masculine. The front left corner is devoted to the Maiden, as represented by Celtic Goddess Brighid. The far left corner is devoted to the Mother, with a shrine to the black Madonna (linked to the Magdalene consciousness and Kali) and a well above, where the ancient witches were initiated. The back right corner, devoted to the horned God, which for me also holds the energy of the Crone.

Glastonbury is one of two places on the planet where the white (masculine) and red (feminine) come together – the other is Mount Shasta in California in the USA. Some say that the White Springs hold the sacred masculine energies while the red springs of the Chalice Well hold the sacred feminine. But to me, and particularly on this day, the White Springs embody the unclaimed feminine – the darker, fierce, wild, powerful parts of us that have been bound and are once more waiting to rise. And in order for us to truly rise and find our true light, we often need to journey dark and deep. Which was exactly why I was there.

As we stood in a circle in front of the main circular well, Lisa initiated the ritual by first calling upon Craig's energy to protect and hold the space. Calling upon the water element pounding around us to assist in moving the energies that were ready to flow, we invoked the Goddess

Magdalene consciousness, subtle beings, and all the women and Priestesses who had come before us doing the work of the feminine. We stated our intention and invited in their support.

Lisa lit the cauldron at the edge of the well, invoking the energy of the dark mother Kali and then began beating her drum. The rhythmic sound reverberating through our bodies and through the entire space felt like the mother's heartbeat vibrating through us in unison. We could feel the energies rising.

One by one we began chanting our own unique songs, inviting the energies to move through us by using our bodies as conduits. Held by the presence of all the women who had ever come together in circle in honor of what is falling away and what is rising, I was overcome with emotion at what was taking place and these three women's ability to allow it to move through them so selflessly. I could feel the Shakti serpent ecstatically weaving through me. Acutely aware of how long it had taken me to journey here and all of the wise women who had supported me along the way, I could feel them, too, standing alongside me.

Amy, Hollie, and Lisa then dispersed to the three corners of the sacred cave and, as a trinity, began to sing their own unique songs. They were not singing, they were being sung. Their voices echoed and hit all the corners of my heart and womb. With an intentional first step, I began my journey from Maiden to Mother to Wise, Wild Woman to Crone in surrender to what was falling away and in deep reverence for what was ready to rise.

Entering the nest of the Maiden, I found Amy surrounded by candles. She invited me to sit with her on a log, under a canopy of branches. Looking into her eyes, I saw my younger self mirrored back. The playful, adventurous, inspired, excitable, big-hearted Maiden so committed and determined to work hard and always do her best.

I was moved to tears as I saw a sadness and depletion in her eyes. From all of the times I had denied her the nourishment and holding she so craved. For pushing her so hard to hurry and grow up. Her young, playful spirit that I had not allowed to roam free. I took her hands and told her how sorry I was for pushing her so hard. For making her feel guilty when she needed to rest. For making her feel like what she was doing was never enough. I told her that I was so sorry for denying and not appreciating this part of myself for so long. I confessed that I knew I needed to move on, but didn't know how to without cutting her off. She took my hand and lovingly led the way.

Feeling the replenished, playful, and joyous strength of the Maiden behind me, I stepped over the threshold toward the Mother. My heart softened and opened wide as Hollie sang, 'Now I walk in beauty. Beauty is before me. Beauty is behind me. Above and below me.'

With mascara all over my face and my flower crown all wonky, I fell into Hollie's arms and allowed myself to be wholly and completely held. Up until that point I didn't realize how much my Maiden had been carrying. Hollie placed my face in her hands and lovingly wiped the tears from my cheeks.

Assisted by the pounding water behind us, I let go of all resistance, allowing my whole body weight to be held by the Mother. While my soul already knew that the Universe held me, it was as if in that moment the human part of me, my body, finally caught up.

Hollie continued singing and rocking me, as if to say, 'I know, I know. Let me hold you. You can rest here.' In her arms, I could feel her voice and heartbeat echoing through my body. And for I have no idea how long, allowed myself to be rocked and nourished by the Great Mother of us all.

I knew that I could retreat to this nurturing nest at any time but now was the time to journey on. I heard the whispers of one of my favorite quotes by Clarissa Pinkola Estés:

**'When a great ship is in harbour and moored,
it is safe, there can be no doubt. But... that
is not what great ships are built for.'**

Seeing that I would prefer to stay in the Mother's nest, but knowing that I was ready Hollie gave me a gentle but firm and encouraging push.

Held by the loving strength and support of my Maiden and Mother, I left the warmth and stepped into my power, as the Wise, Wild Woman. Completely held and nourished by my Maiden and Mother I felt the subtle energy change, as I stepped over yet another threshold back to the front of the well. Something had shifted. I felt strong. Powerful and held in a different way than before.

In front of the well I began to chant and dance, releasing any part of me that was bound up and caged. Shakti surged through me, as I swayed and kicked my wild woman, my too much woman, my ancient wise woman back into my body, made possible by the presence of my three sisters forming a triangle around me.

Just as I finished there was a knock at the door, my signal that it was time to move on, that the outside world was beckoning.

As I made my way around the corner to the depths of the Crone I fell to my knees. My forehead at Lisa's feet, I surrendered to the Crone's wisdom, her potency, her perspective, and capacity not to care about what the world thinks. As I stood back up, she held me in my potency. She placed her hand on my third eye, throat, and then womb, as if to unlock my power as a woman to intuit, speak, and create, and to do so fearlessly.

As we made our way back to the center where it all began, the door flung open and light flooded in. It felt like I had died a hundred deaths and was reborn just as many times. I looked around at my dear sisters, my breath taken from me upon realization that I was not the only one who had been transformed.

Linked by hands, entwined by spirit, our bodies vibrating from what had just taken place.

A pause in our lives where time stood still and the veil got really thin. Breathing deeply, our eyes said all that words could not.

Tourists began flooding in, no idea of the ritual that had just taken place. *Did that really just happen?*

My mind so blown that my legs barely worked. Having to concentrate to put one foot in front of the other. We ventured up Well House Lane, the only word each of us could utter was

'Whoa.'

△

HEALING THE FEMALE LINE

A week later back in Australia, in the lead-up to our wedding, Craig and I hired a wedding planner in an attempt to make sure Mum slowed down and put herself first so she could concentrate on her healing. But she still seemed to be going a million miles an hour, putting everyone before herself.

I was setting up for a one-day retreat. The retreat was down the road from my childhood home and the same location I would be getting married at the next week. Dad arrived to lend a hand and apologized that Mum couldn't be there, as she was resting.

Delighted that Mum was finally putting her own wellbeing first, I cheered inside then heard a crunch, as my left ankle twisted beneath me. Not the best timing when you'll be walking down the aisle in heels six days later. But knowing that the left side of the body represented the female line, I knew there was something bigger at play. After the retreat, I looked at my copy of *You Can Heal Your Life* by Louise Hay and discovered that the ankle represents 'our ability to receive without guilt.'

The next day I hobbled to my hen's party on Sydney Harbor. Having already spoken to Mum about the timing and interpretation of my injury, we were spooked to discover that my half-sister Kylie had injured her left ankle too. If that coincidence was not enough, Nanna Peg then arrived (Mum's mum) and we discovered she had injured her left leg too!

Three generations of women, surrounding my mum, all with the injuries on the left side of their body – the feminine side. The feminine line. Something was happening. I texted my SSS ladies to tell them the news. Their response? 'Whoa.'

△
THE CHAIN

After the wedding, Craig returned to London and I stayed on to spend time with Mum.

On the morning before returning to London I went to Yin Yoga with Mum, Sheila, and Robyn. During the class I discovered the necklace that I wear every single day had broken. On inspection, I noticed that the chain had broken in two leaving a single link lying there free on its own.

After the class Robyn noticed that my necklace was missing. We couldn't see how it could have possibly broken, and yet, one of the links was separate from the chain.

Baffled, the four of us walked across the road to a café. As soon as I sat down I turned to Robyn holding the broken chain and extra link in my hand and said: 'I broke the chain!'

She smiled and nodded, knowing the long journey that had preceded this moment.

With a deep smile, I looked around at this table of courageous wise women who I loved with every corner of my heart. Humbled to be in their presence and deeply grateful, recognizing that this was what I had truly longed for so many years before.

We all got up and walked down to the road to visit Nanna Peg. She had recently had a ministroke and so I sat at her feet holding each of her fingers for a few minutes at a time – an energy healing technique that Sheila had taught me years before – but really, just an excuse for me to hold Nanna's soft hands.

With all of us gathered around her, I asked Nanna to tell us a story from her past. She spoke of the strength of her mother who never gave up hope during the three years that her husband was captured and incarcerated in Changi Prison during World War II and the authorities thought him dead. And the day he walked through the front door. She then spoke of the moment that she discovered her younger brother had committed suicide – of the regrets and the strength of her own mother who lived on without him.

How had I not heard this before? And what else didn't I know?

Four generations of women gathered round, hanging on to her every word. The Great Mother woven through each of us.

Tears rolling down my face, when she finished I thanked her for sharing her story.

She brought her hands to my face, looked at me and said, 'No my darling, the lucky one is me.'

If you slow down enough to notice,
you will find that your life is
made up of such poetry.

If you listen just before the sun
rises, you will hear The Mother
crafting each and every word.

Part II
BIRTHING
A NEW AGE

'They tried to bury us.
They didn't realise we were seeds'

Mexican Proverb

△

WE WERE MADE FOR THESE TIMES

'Do not lose heart... We were made for these times.'
CLARISSA PINKOLA ESTÉS

This is a time of great awakening. The vows of silence have been lifted. We are remembering the sacredness of what it means to be a woman. We are birthing a new age.

The seers and sages of ancient ages predicted this moment of time we are living in. The year 2012 officially marked the beginning, but it has been coming for some time. And you chose to incarnate right in the middle of it. You were made for these times.

Some call it the end of patriarchy. Yogi Bhajan called it, 'the Aquarian Age.' The Mayans call it the 'New Dawn.' I call it the 'Age of Light.' Regardless of what name you give it, all souls are needed to rise up.

Right now we are in a transition period between the ages. In the process of allowing the old cycle to fall away and the new to rise. As with any kind of change, making the transition isn't easy. The things that once served us are falling away. Anything inauthentic is unable to survive. Like driving in the fog and trusting the road will appear before us, we are being forced to release old identities and ways of being that no longer serve us, using our intuition as a compass. If you are reading this book, chances are you are already in the process of doing so and are here to lead the way.

I believe that there is a group of souls who have been incarnating at significant periods of history preparing for this exact time. Devoting their lives to bringing back the voice of the sacred feminine and anchoring her light all over the planet. Reminding the world of the importance of living in harmony with Mother Earth, her seasons, and that healing is possible during periods of history when it was not safe to do so.

Magdalene sisters, daughters of Isis, Essenes, Priestesses, witches, mystics, healers, seers, artists, midwives, visionaries, guardians of the Earth, and storytellers from times past. Interesting women, outspoken women, courageous women, fierce women, women who knew their power, women who trusted their wisdom. And the men who protected Her so She could do Her sacred work. Many were forced to retreat underground in times when it was not safe to share their voice, own their power, and trust their innate wisdom.

This is the dawn of a new day. Ancient feminine wisdom once hidden and silenced, has awakened and is now ready to rise.

Each of us is part of a divine Sisterhood who, by coming together and healing ourselves, will bring about a much-needed shift on the planet. It is time for us all to allow what is beckoning within to be given the permission and space to rise. The process might not be pretty and it quite certainly will not be linear, but it is necessary and it's time.

As one of us awakens and rises, it makes it easier for another to follow her lead.

She is Me and We are She.

Rise Sister Rise.

They went through a lot to be
here together at this time.

There was no way they were going
to sleep through it now.

△

SHAKTI ALWAYS RISES

'True power arises from an inner feminine force – from Shakti.'
SALLY KEMPTON

We each have within us a power. A sacred, creative, feminine force that wants to flow free. Awake in some, dormant in others, always waiting to uncoil and rise.

A life force that is in all things in the Universe, Shakti is the primal spiritual energy located at the base of the spine. Often referred to as Kundalini Shakti and likened to a coiled snake, once activated and awakened it instinctively rises, weaving and spiraling its way up the spine, through each of the chakras to the crown of the head and beyond.

When Shakti begins to rise and move through you, it is easy to feel as though you've developed superpowers. On the one hand you have. On the other, you have merely allowed the sacred feminine creative force of the entire Universe to freely move through you. When your Kundalini Shakti begins to rise your mind is blown, as your remember you are connected to all of Life. You discover that this intelligent force flowing ecstatically through your sacred body is the exact same force that moves through every single living thing.

We can either surrender to the same mysterious feminine force (Shakti) that controls the spinning of the planets, the tides, and the seasons. Or we can continue to struggle and fight and rely on our own separate strength. The choice is ours.

In a hierarchal system, where a few at the top lead the masses, it is not in the interests of those in power to have so many tapped into such an infinite power. It is our power (Shakti) that patriarchy endeavored to control. The part of us that knows that we are connected to all. That we have the same sacred force within us that causes flowers to open, the tides to rise and fall. That I am, you are, we all are sacred and divine. Many ancient traditions see women as the providers of Shakti, as you'll discover later in Herstory (see page 67).

The Mayans and other ancient civilizations predicted that the world would end in some way in 2012, as their calendars don't go beyond December 21. As you are reading this book, clearly it was not the end of the world, rather a marking of the end of the world as we knew it, and the coming of a new age. While the specific dates vary, it is believed that around the time of 2012, the Earth transitioned from the Piscean Age into the Aquarian Age. From the Dark Ages to the Age of Light. With the coming of this new age, many began to experience their Kundalini Shakti beginning to rise.

Some of the physical side effects of a Kundalini Shakti awakening are involuntary jerks or shaking, heat, visions, periods of euphoria, depression, and energy rushes. Through working with Shakti, you can begin to release ways that you have kept your power contained. You can free yourself to flow more effortlessly with all of Life.

This divine feminine force is once again taking Her place. As each of us surrenders to Her rising, we are in effect embodying the sacred power, ancient wisdom, and unconditional love that this planet has been starved of for so long.

RISE SISTER RISE

Did you experience an awakening of
sorts around the year of 2012?

Have you experienced your Kundalini Shakti awakening
or experienced any of the side effects described above?

△

THE HOLY GRAIL IS WITHIN YOU

In many ancient traditions, woman is seen as the provider of Shakti – of the spiritual life force that connects all of Life. In short: Unconditional love. That's what the pure balanced feminine is made of. That is the potent power of She.

Shakti is the divine feminine creative power. An unstoppable force that is available to flow through every woman. The hangover of patriarchy has left us feeling that there is something wrong with our bodies but nothing can be further from the truth. There is a sacred vibrational field within a woman's womb that we have forgotten. The ancients knew it (*hello Priestesses of Isis*) and it is time that we reclaim it.

Your body is holy. Your sexuality is holy. You are holy. May we unshackle ourselves from seeing ourselves as anything but this.

Every woman is a Goddess, for she has the capacity to embody the divine feminine Shakti in full radiant force.

The flower uses Shakti to attract the bee, and women have been shamed for being like that flower. Shakti is power and in a patriarchal society where one controls many, a woman in her power doesn't mix well. And so for many this energetic connection has been severed. Now is the time for us to heal it.

When my husband and I first connected, I was fully in my feminine. Having experienced my second Kundalini Shakti awakening (*see page 17*), I found myself for the first time in my life 'in love' – not with anyone but with life itself. I was in a space of pure unconditional love.

My inner chalice was full. I was a woman one-in-herself. I didn't long for anything outside for I was connected to the Source of all.

Having been through his own transformation, Craig was in his masculine and in deep respect of the sacred feminine. Without warning, as we came together in sacred union, the sacred Shakti intertwined between us in an ecstasy that was far more than sex. Blown away by the experience, the very next day Craig decided to name his contracting company 'Kundalini Ltd.'

May we all release the internal dialogue that tells us our bodies are anything but holy. May we reject any external force that suggests we should be anything other than the shape and size we are. May we lovingly nurse ourselves back to adoring every ounce of our flesh. Every woman is radiant. May we fiercely reject anything that suggests otherwise.

#RISESISTERRISE MANTRA

I allow Shakti to flow freely through me. I am open to unleashing the potency of my sexuality and embrace it all as a holy act. May my inner chalice always be full.

RISE SISTER RISE

What have you been programmed to believe about your body and sexuality?

△

RETURNING

In order to thrive in the Age of Light, we must fall back into flow with the cyclic nature of Life. To do this we must move from a 'me' focus to a 'we' focus, and remember that all of Life is part of a larger whole. We are not separate from the Earth, rather we are part of it. We are the ones that run the risk of not surviving, if we don't heed Her calls.

It is no coincidence that you are here on the planet right now, that you too have chosen to return at this stage in history, or that this book landed in your hands. May these pages act as an activation, a transmission, an unveiling, an unleashing, a remembering of what you came here to do, and all that you came here to share. With every page that you turn, may we together release any way in which we have learned to keep our feminine power, voice, magic, wisdom, creativity, and light dimmed. May we heal any resistance to, or disconnection from, the Shakti that wants to flow through each and every part of Life. May we release any vows of silence and layers of protection. May we see our sensitivities and intuitive nature as our strengths. May we heal the separation and shadow of patriarchy that exists in the world and within ourselves. May we bow down to the flow of Life and receive all that is wanting to be created through us. May we stop persecuting each other.

Finally, may we together heal our inner worlds so that our outer one – our magnificent planet Earth – can continue to be the place we call home.

RISE SISTER RISE

Are you ready to surrender to the same force that
controls the spinning of the planets or are you still
invested in your own control and strength?

△

THE MYSTERY OF WOMAN

*'Women are the leaders of the Aquarian Age not because
they have finally "won" the proverbial war of the sexes, but
because they have finally recognized their own true nature
and decided to serve it – and deliver it – for the good of all.'*

YOGI BHAJAN

Woman are not taught, they awaken. Every woman has a mysterious force within her. An ancient wisdom that is always whispering. A rhythmic flow that is not only connected to the life force of the planet but the entire Universe. A cyclic nature, that if all women surrendered to, the whole planet would come back into balance.

A divine power as fierce as the tides, as great as the mountains, as wild as the jungle, as mysterious as the moonlight and as bright as the sun. A holy force that has been contained and restrained for millennia, but is ready again to rise.

Many of us have experienced a loss of contact with the mysterious powers of being a woman, in our efforts to fit into a linear model. Trying to make it in a man's world. It's time to release the bindings that keep us restrained, to bow down to the Mother and let her rhythms beat us home. We must heal the insecurities inherited from patriarchy that keep us caged. It is time to reclaim our connection with Shakti (power), innate wisdom (intuition), and ferocious, unconditional love. When we do this, nothing will be able to stop Her from rising.

RISE SISTER RISE

What is rising in you?

Δ

WHEN ONE WOMAN HEALS

'Every woman who heals herself helps heal all the women
who came before her and all those who will come after.'
DR. CHRISTIANE NORTHRUP

It's easy to look at the state of the planet right now and get overwhelmed. To feel that there is nothing that we could possibly do to turn it around. But I don't believe that is true. Every tiny effort affects the greater whole. It is never ever too late.

The tragedies of the Earth right now are due to our separation. The way we treat Her is a reflection of how we treat ourselves. The only way to heal the world around us is by first healing ourselves. The more we focus on self-healing, the more chance we have to heal this breathtakingly beautiful planet we are so blessed to call home.

To heal means to make whole. The process of healing brings us back into balance with the whole of Life. Therefore, when one woman heals she doesn't just heal herself, rather she heals the larger whole. When one woman heals and brings herself back into harmony, she sends out ripples. To those who came before her and those who will come afterward. She can never truly know the impact, but she can be sure that her personal healing will not just be felt by her. As she is brought into harmony, the whole planet is too.

This work of self-healing isn't easy. It requires that we unearth our shadow and sit with it. It's uncomfortable, which is why not everyone does it. Numbing ourselves out is much easier. The fact that you are consciously working on your own personal healing is something that is both courageous and admirable. You are a leader just by doing so. Thank you for wanting to do it.

RISE SISTER RISE

What are you being called to heal?

What have you been avoiding healing?

What is the first baby step in healing this/these things now?

$\triangle$

A NEW PARADIGM OF CHANGE

We are entering a new paradigm, going from one age to the next. Which means that the linear rules we once built our lives on (the systems and identities that once served us) are all changing. Updating. Recalibrating. We need to allow ourselves to be moved by the changes. To be fluid, not rigid, regimented, and set.

The old ways of waiting until it gets too much to withstand and then doing a complete life overhaul are over. Of building the tower as high as we can and being overwhelmed that it must fall. We must listen and allow ourselves to be transformed, little by little, as it happens.

When we surrender to the rhythm of Life, we find a new way of being where we learn to dance with uncertainty and be moved and supported by the cosmic intelligence of Shakti. Not mourning the loss of the sun, rather appreciating the glow of the moon. Not missing the stillness of night, rather celebrating the coming dawn.

Aligning your life is a never-ending process. It is a day-by-day, moment-to-moment practice. Not a one-off overhaul. Living a life of alignment is a daily practice. Checking in, staying on course, redirecting as you travel. Noticing what feels good, free, and spacious, and what feels restrictive, stagnant, and stuck. What is falling away and what is ready to rise.

At present there is a lot of fast-moving high-vibrational energy hitting the Earth and the Earth is changing at a cellular level. As it does our physical and emotional bodies attune to this frequency – we are part of the Earth after all. Just as when glass is put under high-vibrational pressure it shatters, we too are the same. Old identities and ways of being that once served us are no longer able to survive.

Let the shattering occur, for the shattering allows the pieces to rearrange all by themselves.

RISE SISTER RISE

What in your life feels stagnant and stuck?

Δ

THE NEVER-ENDING PROCESS OF RISING

'She did not find the grim in falling apart. For every
time she found herself broken, she knew she was
brutally remaking herself, and collapsing to be
reborn like a rioting star; haunting the dark sky.'
R.M. DRAKE

Rising is uncomfortable. And in many cases it ain't pretty. Fairytales and movies glorify the process. Suggesting that there is an end point to get to, a happily ever after where all of our ducks are perfectly lined up in a row. A place to arrive at once you've overcome a particular hurdle or series of challenges that once stood in your way. A ladder to climb. A mountain to conquer. A person to forgive. A relationship to get over. An award to strive for. And once you have finally achieved this momentous thing. Once you get commissioned as an artist. Published as an author. Find and marry your true love. Heal the ailment in your body. Conceive a child. Stop compulsively eating. Once you truly awaken. You will have finally arrived and things will then be amazing. Your real life can start. At last.

And then, when we finally get what we want, we do all that we can to hold on to it. It is at this exact moment that we fall out of flow with Life. Like the wheel of Life that never stops turning, the longer you cling on and try to stay where you were, the more out of flow with Life you get.

Life is not linear, it's cyclic. A boundless journey of transformation. Of highs and lows. Of joys and sadness. Of contraction and expansiveness. Of birth and death. Of wins and losses. Change is a sure thing. Our ability to surrender to its natural rhythms is our greatest tool.

No day is better or worse, both have much richness to offer – the days when we rise and the ones when we fall. The sign of a true soul pilgrim is that when the brittle winds slap Her face, somewhere deep down there is an inner voice within whispering that this experience is good too. If we are here to rise and grow and expand and lead, then the challenging times aren't worse than the celebratory ones.

If we fall it doesn't mean that we have failed, rather it is another invitation to transform and expand.

There's a lesson in every battle, in every struggle, in every 'what the hell do you want me to do now?' And often it is the same, unforgiving wind that encourages us to effortlessly sail.

Rising is not linear but an endless cycle. Allowing it to change us takes courage, which is why most people resist it. You are not most people.

RISE SISTER RISE

What in your life is falling away?

What in your life has an expiry date?

When She realized that
She was living through it,
She let go of the need to understand it
And used her

heart

as   a

compass.

△

TRANSFORMATION AND RECALIBRATION

The whole process of transforming is pretty miraculous. It quite literally means to change form, nature, and appearance. With all of the leaps in awakening and consciousness that stepping into a new age requires, we are each going through a massive recalibration. Changing both our physical form and our vibrational frequency.

In this life, changing at soul level is pointless if you don't give your physical body time to embody the transformation. To hold the shift at cellular level as well as emotional, mental, and soul level. As we release attachments, identities, and old ways of being, our body too needs time to clear these things from our systems. Be compassionate and watch on in awe, as your miraculous body recalibrates to assist you.

If you don't allow the time and space to incorporate the change, the higher frequency can't be held in the body. The rise in consciousness is stuck in thought. All air. No ground. Leaving you to grasp and try and hold on, as the winds of time continue to blow.

This is not the time to have spiritual conversations.
This is the time to DO the work.

Just as the redwood that longs to rise toward the light must first drop her roots deep, so must we. She cannot grow tall without that anchoring, without being held by the Earth. If your body requires naps and rest while reading this book, honor that. Just because you're doing nothing doesn't mean your body isn't doing something miraculous.

In the lead-up to and while writing this book, I've been going through my own sort of recalibration. I've been sick several times. Some days after finishing a chapter, out of nowhere I need to take a nanna nap. I've been honoring these calls, which quite honestly have been extremely challenging, especially with deadlines looming. I even requested a one-month extension a few months back, feeling it was necessary if I was to be able to embody the message that this book demanded.

We are being called to soften in order to strengthen, to drop our roots deep in order to rise high. Give yourself the rest and recuperation necessary for the transformation process to happen in full. Allow time to reroute and rewire.

Ask the butterfly. After it has eaten and grown all it can, it builds a cocoon. At a glance the caterpillar appears to be just chilling out and resting, but in reality, nothing could be further from the truth. Inside, the caterpillar is rapidly transforming.

It is actually during this resting phase that it is most productive. While it is cocooned in its sac, it is quite literally changing form! Organs, limbs, tissues, the whole deal – all parts of the caterpillar are changing. Interrupt this process too soon and the butterfly would be completely unformed. But wait in faith for just a moment; in between your breaths, something completely new and breathtaking will be born.

We need to change our belief that in order to be productive we need to be busy. To allow the wisdom of our bodies to do what they do best. To believe that the Universe and all of Life is supporting our constant transformation. Life is weaving, regardless of what we are doing.

The moment we get in the way or try to micromanage the Universe, we mess up the magnificent order of Life. Nature has an innate intelligence that knows exactly what to do. You are part of nature. So you do too.

RISE SISTER RISE

Are you honoring your body's calls to allow
this transformation to happen?

△

OF ALL THAT FALLS AND RISES AND RISES AND FALLS

We are in a constant state of rising and falling.

Falling and rising.

All and everything we must do is allow what is

Falling to fall away and what is rising to rise.

Life is circular like that.

You can either rise and fall with it

Or resist and struggle against it.

The part of you that can never die

Is forever whispering stories of letting go.

You can surrender to the same force that controls the whole cosmos

Or rely on the fading strength of your separateness.

You can listen to Her whispers or you can

Wait for the tower to fall.

△

SHATTERING TO SET YOURSELF FREE

In order for the new to arrive, we must first allow the old to shatter. Sometimes this happens on its own. And sometimes it requires that we do the smashing. To tear apart what we've built because things have changed, including you. To admit that while it once was aligned, now it no longer is. This shattering requires both courage and faith. Courage to let go and faith that the pieces will come back together again in a way that is more aligned than it was before.

RISE SISTER RISE

What part of your life needs to be shattered
in order to set yourself free?

△
A NEW MATRIX

We live in a system that says we are not enough and so we are constantly striving to be something other than what we are. A system that tells us that anything that is outside of me is valuable. But that is just not true.

When you realize that what is truly precious is either already within you or coming to you, striving is no longer necessary.

When you realize that never-ending achievement doesn't bring you what you're searching for, it is revolutionary. For it leads you to a place where there is nothing you need outside of who you truly are. You are out of the matrix; you are able to unplug.

There is no external vision or model for what is ahead. We are the ones who are called to create that. We cannot look anywhere except for within ourselves for that.

This is the power of the wise woman. She knows that she has everything she needs within herself and that she has the power to create and birth life both within and outside her body. Can you feel it? A new future is being born.

RISE SISTER RISE

What are you being called to unplug from?

What new path or way of doing things
are you being called to forge?

△

WITH EVERY NEW BREATH

With every new breath she created a new matrix for herself.

A matrix this time so strong that it was impossible
to be penetrated by those around her:

By inherited patterns of stories told both to her, by her, and about her.

A matrix so fierce that it didn't matter what was

Thrown her way, for now she drew her power and truth

From an untouchable unwavering place that resided deep within.

With every new exhale she released lifetimes of oppression.

Of enforced power. Of pain and suffering. Of guilt and shame.

Of holding back Her voice, Her truth, Her wisdom,

Her knowingness, Her powerfulness, Her holiness.

Of holding things in Her body that were not even Hers.

She was born in the fire.

Each new flame igniting an untamable power
that could never be extinguished.

Not now. Not ever.

With every new breath she created a new matrix for herself.

And when She was done,

She looked around and found Herself in a sea of sisters.

Who this whole time, had been doing the exact same thing.

△

RECLAIMING HERSTORY, AND THE SHADOW OF PATRIARCHY

God has been considered to be female for much longer than She has been considered male. Ancient Mother God worship (often referred to as the Old Religion) dates back more than 35,000 years, making it more ancient than Christianity, Buddhism, Hinduism, Islam, and Judaism.

Honoring Mother God

Cave paintings, carvings, and sacred art honoring the cyclic nature of the female body and worship of Mother God have been found in prehistoric caves and sites throughout Europe and the East.

Cave paintings dating back more than 35,000 years shine a light on what is thought to be the earliest depiction of Mother God worship.

During the last Ice Age humans were forced to surrender to the power of Mother Earth. It is thought that hunters and gatherers would connect with the spirit of the Earth and the animals in order to survive such brutal conditions.

Women's bodies were seen as sacred and women as Goddesses because they quite literally give birth to Life. We all came from woman. The planet was seen as feminine (Mother Earth). Our menstrual cycle connected to the phases of the moon (*as described later on page 114*), our ancestors marking the moon's phases through etching into bone. People lived in accordance with the Earth's natural rhythms and cycles, and thus in harmony with all of Life.

Everything was considered sacred: Plants, animals, the Earth itself, and men and women alike. Those who could connect deeply with the spirit of nature were revered as shamans and Priestesses.

As the ice began to melt and the temperature got milder, ley lines were discovered (powerful energetic paths underneath the Earth's surface). Sacred stone circles and temples were built on the ley lines as places of ritual and worship. The warmer weather saw tribes turning into communities as travel was now possible. Some tribes migrated to the Americas and settled there. All stages of womanhood were honored as depicted in the worship of the Triple Goddess. Women transitioned from Maiden, to Mother, to Wise Woman/Crone. In many Mother God societies, wealth and property were passed on through the female line with men taking the female name as their own when they married.

Healers were highly revered, working in harmony with nature, using herbs to treat ailments. Midwives welcomed and ushered in new life with sacred reverence. High Priestesses devoted their lives to honoring Mother God and her elements on behalf of all people. Seers were called upon for guidance and Wise Women were highly revered as wisdom keepers crucial for embodying and passing on the knowledge of life.

The Bronze and Iron Ages saw nomadic tribes devoted to the arts of war invading and conquering many of the Mother God-worshiping cultures of Europe, Africa, the Middle East, and India.

Women were raped, enslaved, and forced to marry, thus extinguishing the matrilineal lines. In her book *The Spiral Dance*, Starhawk describes:

> *In Greece the Goddess, in her many guises, 'married' the new Gods – the result was the Olympian Pantheon. In the British Isles, the victorious Celts adopted many features of the Mother God Religion, incorporating them into Druidic mysteries.*

Christianity and Mother Mary

With the introduction of Christianity, churches were built in honor of Mother Mary, who became for many, another way of worshiping Mother God. Many Mother God worshipers and High Priestesses who refused to marry took vows of celibacy and became nuns. They continued their worship of the Mother in the safest way they knew – by worshiping Mother Mary.

The Roman Empire began using Christianity as a political means to control the masses. Empowered women (and men) who saw themselves and the Earth as sacred were forced to convert and worship an external all-powerful external solo male God. Those who didn't conform were branded 'pagans' by the Roman Empire, which historically means, belonging or relating to a religion that worships many gods, especially one that existed before the world's main religions. Many Mother God temples and places of worship were conquered, as can be seen in images of St Michael slaying the dragon/snake – the dragon/snake representing the rising Shakti energy (serpent of the Goddess) and the sin of women – in many churches.

A woman's sacred body went from being a sacred vessel to the property of man. Sexual urges of both men and women were seen as sinful, disconnecting us from our bodies. Women were forced to fit into two archetypes (the Virgin aka the 'good girl,' and the 'whore.')

In their book *The Great Cosmic Mother*, Monica Sjöö and Barbara Mor explain the origin of the word 'Virgin':

> *'Virgin' meant not married, not belonging to a man – a woman who was 'one-in-herself'. The very word derives from a Latin root meaning strength, force, skill; and was later applied to men. Ishtar, Diana, Astarte, Isis were all called Virgin, which did not refer to sexual chastity, but sexual independence.*

Stories of the sacred feminine were changed to worship the masculine. Worship of the Maiden, Mother, and Crone were replaced with worship of the Father, Son, and Holy Ghost. The powerful darker sides of the feminine were extinguished from society.

Sacred texts and scrolls of ancient mystic teachings including those of Mother God and Goddess worship were both suppressed and destroyed, most notably with the fire in the Great Library of Alexandria – one of the most significant libraries of the ancient world.

Mother God worship is also referred to as natural witchcraft, drawing its teachings from the cycles, power and wisdom of nature (Mother God). The term witch derived from the word *wicce*, which means 'wise,' thus 'witchcraft' meaning 'craft of the wise.'

The witch hunts

The Inquisition began in the 12th century as a way of enforcing control, with many Christian sects such as the Cathars being accused of heresy. Witchcraft was deemed a heretical act, with women such as Joan of Arc being burned at the stake on May 30, 1431. In 1484 Pope Innocent VIII pronounced a Papal Bull against witchcraft and the witch hunts and trials would continue until the 17th century.

In 1486, the book *Malleus Maleficarum* ('Hammer of the Witches') by Heinrich Kramer, a German Catholic clergyman, was published and would soon be by the side of every judge during the witch trials. During this time, the accused were attached to ducking stools and submerged in city rivers as a holy test. If they sank it meant that they were innocent and in fact not a witch (because they were now dead). If they survived, it confirmed that they were witches, in which case they would be baptized by fire and burned at the stake while people looked on.

Fear controlled the villages of Europe and parts of the Americas as their inhabitants were forced to watch the guilty 'witches/pagans' burn in front of them. Women were tortured and forced to sit on burning iron stools because their sexuality was considered satanic.

It was impossible to protect others or speak out against the terrorism for fear of being accused of heresy and given an unfair trial, and suffering an excruciating death. It is impossible to find a definitive figure of how many people were killed during the witch hunts, but estimates range from tens of thousands to many millions. The BBC recently reported that 900 'witches" bodies were found buried below a church in Aberdeen, Scotland, having been sentenced to death for crimes such as 'healing cattle.' The accused were not given fair trials and it is likely that most were not given trials at all. Monica Sjöö and Barbara Mor describe in their book, *The Great Cosmic Mother*, how it is believed that 80 percent of people sentenced to death for witchery at this time were women.

One of the most devastating things about this period of history is that it caused women to turn against each other as they were tortured until they named their accomplices in witchcraft, causing, I believe, a deep mistrust between women that still can be felt today.

Modern-day Goddess worship

Today, Goddess worship can be found in all corners of the Earth – India to Egypt, the British Isles to China, Greece to the Middle East, Turkey to Tibet. Goddesses such as Durga, Kali, Kwan Yin, Tara, Isis, Horus, Vega, Parvati, Mazu, Brighid, Danu, Morgan, Shakti, Selene, Ishtar, Hebat, Tefnut, Naunet, Artemis, Aphrodite, Hera, Demeter. The sacred feminine may have changed form, but She has never truly left.

We have come a long way and there is further for us to go in order to heal the wounds and soul rememberings of the past.

**This might be the story of Her fall. But we
are living in the time of Her rise.**

**Through the winds, the trees and the
beating of our hearts She whispers:**

'Rise Sister Rise.'

△
A PRAYER FOR HER RISING

As we shake off the shackles of the past, may we create a
whole new archetype for women in these awakening times.

As we reclaim our voices, may we find the strength
to speak for those who do not have one.

As we surrender to our cyclic nature may we be
strengthened by the effortless rhythm of the Earth.

As we honor our bodies, may we be reconnected
with the ancient wisdom that lies within.

As we remember the sacredness of our womanhood may
we step into the potency of who we came here to be.

As we let go of mistrust and past hurts, may we mend
the severing of sisterhood and remember that there
is more than enough room for us all to rise.

And so it is. And so it is. And so it is.

Δ

She realized that the
worst patriarchy was the
patriarchy She was
enforcing within Herself.

△

BALANCING THE MASCULINE AND FEMININE IN YOU

*'I believe in the power of men who respect
the Earth and her women.'*
Rune Lazuli

We each have within us both masculine and feminine energies. While your sex indicates what energies you chose to focus on in this life, we still embody both.

As we are coming out of 5,000 years of patriarchy, where the unbalanced masculine has been the focus, it is important to note that the unbalanced feminine can be just as destructive.

Just as the sacred feminine's anger has been silenced through patriarchy, the sacred masculine's ability to express emotion and recognize his divinity has too.

As we recover from patriarchy, it is important not to aspire to its polar opposite – patriarchy to matriarchy. Rather, let's bring the sacred masculine and sacred feminine energies back into balance. As the sacred feminine rises, may the sacred masculine rise along with Her.

Below is a list of some of the characteristics of the sacred masculine and feminine energies when balanced and unbalanced. Read through and see which you relate to; remember we are capable of them all.

SACRED FEMININE	UNBALANCED FEMININE
Compassionate, wise, in touch with her ability to heal, connected with nature and her seasons, sees herself as whole, loves unconditionally, fiercely protective of the planet and her children, sexual, wise, knows her power, intuitive, passionate, empathetic, understanding, healer, fertile, creative, abundant, in flow with the rest of life, provider of Shakti, assertive, truth seeker, fills up her well, able to be supported, revered and adored by the masculine, able to express anger and passion	Depressed, needy, codependent, overly sensitive, wallowing and self-pitying, bitter, self-doubting, victim, people-pleaser, the good girl, low self-esteem, dependent, unable to stand on own two feet, gossip, resentful, doesn't want to be happy, martyr, selfish, can't stand other people's happiness, manipulative, scheming, controlling, spiteful, unable to express her needs, insecure, puts everyone else's needs ahead of her own, in thought compares self to others

SACRED MASCULINE	UNBALANCED MASCULINE
Strong, protective, worships the feminine, supportive, present, active, proactive, abundant, powerful, provider, confident, physical, energized, passionate, heroic, courageous, able to be supported by the feminine, able to surrender to and be held by the feminine, able to love unconditionally, in touch with feelings but doesn't let them control him, empowered, not threatened	Destroys everything in his/her path, ruthless, does not think of anyone but himself, the end justifies the means, forceful, brutal, barbaric, selfish, egoistic, sees him/herself as separate, arrogant, disconnected, from the head up, weak, cruel, disconnected from emotions, easily threatened, cowardly, deceitful, stubborn, endures and strives when it is time to rest, headstrong

△

GOODBYE TO THE GOOD GIRL

'As a woman I am expected to want everything
to be nice, and to be nice myself... I don't design
nice buildings – I don't like them.'
ZAHA HADID

Patriarchy tells us that if we follow a linear model everything will work out. Do long hours, keep your head down, just stick at it, you will be rewarded in the end.

The old rules of pushing on through for some promise or reward in the future no longer apply. Rugs are being pulled and whatever is inauthentic is becoming harder to hold on to. It is in these times that Kali, the dark mother, is by our side beckoning for us to loosen our grip, and let go, let go, let go. To let the Earth's natural rhythm and our own medicine call us home.

This isn't to say that you shouldn't have a strong work ethic or fight for something that you love, but don't push on through or fight for it blindly because that is what you *should do* or because you fear not having it in your life. We must no longer be enslaved and caged by our fears.

Do it because it's what you desire. Do it because it brings you pleasure. Do it because it makes you come alive. Do it because it lights you up. Do it because your intuition told you to. Do it because it ignites a spark in your heart. Do it because it lights a fire between your legs. Do it because it's what you came here to do.

We must relinquish our people-pleasing patterns. We must stop all endeavors to be the good girl who blindly follows and does what she is told. We must turn our authority within using our intuition as our compass.

We must rise as women not follow as girls.

Forget what *they* will say. If *they* gossip, it's a sure sign you are doing something noticeable and good. Forge the path. Leave dust behind you. Have the courage to live your life in full.

Remember the description of 'Virgin' (*see page 69*) as being a woman 'one-in-herself.' Ancient Priestesses were seen as Virgins: Independent sovereign women who could not be owned or bound. When you reclaim your Priestess power you cease needing to be the 'good girl' and you step into your womanhood. You step into being a woman one-in-herself. Which you already are. So be that. Reclaim that. Initiate yourself as that.

RISE SISTER RISE

If you weren't afraid of what other people would think, say, or do what would you do?

How are you trying to people-please or be the good girl in your life?

How can you reclaim your Priestess power and be a woman one-in-herself?

△

LET'S BURN THE ARCHETYPES

As I alluded to earlier, for far too long women have been limited to two socially acceptable archetypes: the Virgin (the good girl) and the Mother (nurturing, loving, protective, and selfless) with no room for anything in between. Women are either Madonnas or whores. Good girls or bitches. Holy or witches.

The hangover of all of this has resulted in us doing our best to fit into these two acceptable archetypes and feeling shameful for all the bits that spill over the edges. The practice of endeavoring to keep our shadow side contained must come to an end. If we deny our shadow, we deny our light in all its power. From the ashes of the fire, the phoenix She rises.

We cannot truly be free if we are doing all that we can to keep a certain part of us hidden. Keeping the Wild Woman restrained in fear of the threat of being branded a 'bitch' or 'whore' needs to stop.

'Good girls' go through life pushing down rage, pushing down desire, pushing down shame, pushing down anger, pushing down the shadow, pushing down so much of the natural, wonderful, pleasurable, passionate, potent, and powerful parts of being a woman. When we are doing all we can to keep all of that contained, it's no wonder we may find ourselves having 'bitchy' or even so called 'whore-like' outbursts. It is not possible to be the good girl all the time. It's not healthy either. When we attempt to do so we cut ourselves off from the potent power of being a woman. The world needs more women, and fewer women as little girls.

But what if we took the shame and fear out of it? What if we saw our raw, wild, crazy, completely natural Shakti energy in all her embodiments and expressions as sacred? What if we reclaimed the dark parts of the lunar cycle and created space for all of Her to be here – to embrace the fierce Kali, Durga, and Lalita parts of our feminine nature? What if we saw all parts of the feminine as holy? What if every woman tapped into her potent power and innate wisdom? What if every woman chose to rise? We would start a (r)evolution, that's what.

RISE SISTER RISE

How are you keeping yourself contained?

Where in your life do you resort to being a little girl instead of a powerful woman?

How can you let more of your crazy, wild, passionate, sexual, fierce, powerful self out?

Her rising
started a (r)evolution.

△

YOU DON'T GET TO SAY WHO I AM

The media and the world around us are constantly trying to tell us who we are. If you don't know who you are with conviction, you will crumble and conform to what society says about you. Your true nature will be stifled. That would be a tragic shame. You are a walking piece of art. Crafted for lifetimes. Don't waste it by letting others define you.

Be the author of your life. Claim who you are in all of your potency now.

In order to allow our true nature the space and nourishment it needs to rise, we must be vigilant at creating an intimate relationship with ourselves. We must study ourselves. Become experts in You©. If others have an opinion of you, it is simply that – an opinion, theirs. An opinion tainted by the filter that they see the world through. As a change-maker, you are choosing to see the world in a different way. Most people are not like you. Change-makers change things. Change is uncomfortable.

We must be relentless in the reclamation of who we are so that when another comes with their judgments (and they will, especially when you're forging a path), you are so secure in your core identity that no words or amount of energy can throw you off your course. No one gets to say who you are but you.

RISE SISTER RISE

Who do people see you as or say you
are that is just not accurate?

Who have you learned to be that is not actually who you are?

Who are you really?

△

It was in the ashes
that she found her phoenix.
And boy was it worth the wait.

△

OWN WHO YOU ARE

'I am not who I sleep with. I am not my weight.
I am not my mother. I am myself.'
AMY SCHUMER

You cannot stand in your power unless you know who you are and own it. The strengths and the weaknesses, the shadow and the light.

If you don't know who you are and claim it, you will look to others for permission to be who you think you might be or desire to be someday.

If you know who you are with conviction, no one can define your worth, take away your power, bring you down, or say what is possible but you.

If you own your shadow no one can call you out, for you would have already claimed it.

So who are you? Write a list of ten things that are true about your light and your shadow. Light and dark. Own it ALL. Shame-free.

THE LIGHT (THE GOOD)   THE DARK (THE SHADOW)

And on a morning no
different from any other

She met herself in the mirror
She met herself in the mirror

And quite liked
What She saw.

△

EMBRACING YOUR 'TOO MUCH'

'The world needs your medicine, woman.'
SARAH DURHAM WILSON

Do not underestimate the power of reclaiming your so-called weaknesses. With the right understanding, these can be the most precious things of all. More often than not, our weaknesses are actually the exact things that are masking our unique gifts. Our unique gifts aren't meant to fit perfectly into a linear world – that's why they are unique.

Think of the parts of you that you've tried to fit into a box. The times you've been accused of being 'too much' of something. *Too sensitive, too emotional, too sexual, too opinionated, too honest, too blunt, too big...* This 'too much' is just a way of saying your uniqueness is different and makes me feel uncomfortable.

Say you are someone who is 'too sensitive.' Perhaps you are drained by crowds and being around other people constantly and thus crave free time on your own. Perhaps when you don't give yourself this solitude, you are quite grumpy, people call you selfish or rude or whatever. So you try to endure this craving for solitude, in order to fit in with the rest of life. To bind up the thing that you are 'too much' of. In doing this, this unique thing about you becomes the thing that you need to 'overcome.'

But what if this so-called weakness was actually your strength. What if this craving for solitude was actually your medicine? What if by giving yourself the medicine that you so crave you stumble upon your true gift to the world? What if your sensitivity [*or insert your 'too much thing' here*] was not something that needed fixing, rather, it was your gift? What if it was the solitude that filled you up and allowed you to do the work that you are here to do?

What if your so-called weakness was actually your greatest gift?

In the wrong setting – for example working in an open-plan office – sensitivity and need for solitude could be seen as a weakness. But in the right setting, say spending your days creating, your weakness could actually be your unique gift. And by giving yourself the medicine that you crave, this unique gift can then be alchemized into medicine for the world.

In the wrong setting – for example working for an unethical corporation – your highly opinionated, truth-speaking nature gets you into trouble. But in the right setting, say forging a new way of ethical leadership using your art to have the conversation you want to have with the world, your weakness could actually be seen as a gift.

Before I stepped into my current work, being a healer, spiritual teacher and writer, I saw myself as being 'too sensitive' or 'feeling things too much.' But, since realigning my entire life around my true nature and giving myself the medicine I need, these so-called weaknesses are actually now my greatest strengths.

My sensitivity allows me to write from the heart and to pick up on the slightest subtleties in my clients' energy, to empathize and deeply relate. My craving for solitude was a craving for the very thing that nourishes my true nature. The solitude was my medicine. And by honoring this, my medicine is transmuted into medicine for others. When I am nourished by the solitude I am able to feel and hear the words that are mine to share – to allow my writing and creations to flow through me. Today my whole business is built on my so-called weaknesses on those parts of me that were 'too much.'

What makes you different from others?
What parts of you have you been trying to change
in order to fit into a box-shaped world?

If you inquire deeply enough, you may just discover that your greatest weakness may in fact be your greatest strength. And in living in service to that, your true medicine will be transformed into medicine for others.

RISE SISTER RISE

What have you been accused of being 'too much'
of: Too sensitive, too opinionated, too sexual,
too passionate, too emotional, too honest, too
much of a big presence, too disillusioned...?

This is your unique strength.

What does this unique strength demand
from you in order to nurture it?

This is your medicine.

How can you realign your life so that your medicine
could be alchemized into medicine for the world?

This is your gift to the world.

My unique strength is...

My medicine is...

My gift to the world is...

△

IT'S OK TO SOFTEN

You don't need to suffer in order to succeed. You don't need to strive in order to make things happen. You don't need to hold it all together. You will become stronger, as you soften. You will be more supported, as you stop pushing so hard. When we loosen our grip what is truly meant for us will stay, that which isn't will go.

Many of us have learned to rise in a man's world. Learned to be skilled at things that are not aligned to our core. Each time we do these things we lose a little bit of ourselves. The tighter we hold on to an old way of being, the more rigid life gets and the more likely the tower will come crumbling down.

The days of fitting into a linear model in order to survive are coming to an end. We must soften back into our true nature and call all the lost pieces back. In softening to our true nature, we will each forge a new path without even trying.

RISE SISTER RISE

What are you trying to control or bend to your will?

What have you learned to be good at that drains you?

What are you striving for/where in your
life are you pushing or controlling?

What is behind that striving/pushing/controlling?

How are you being called to soften?

DIVINE MOTHER

Thank you for assisting me in
releasing any old identities that are no longer aligned
with who I am and came here to be.

While I acknowledge and appreciate
how they have served me thus far,
I stand here willing to release my
attachment to them so that even more of
my true nature can emerge.

And so It Is.

△

OLD IDENTITIES AND WHAT'S NO LONGER SUSTAINABLE

We are all being called to face up to those parts of our lives that are no longer sustainable.

To methods of survival, which might have served us tremendously in the past, but now have an expiry date.

To learned ways of being that no longer have our best interests at heart.

To those parts of our soul's shadow we allow to define who we are.

To identities that are out of alignment with who we are today, or that we no longer need.

As we are called to transform, it is crucial that we get clear on what identities we are leaving behind so that we change the program, as well as the circumstances. I am ready to let go of being the one who puts service to others ahead of service to herself, the one who overschedules her day so she always feels like she is not getting enough done, the one who is driven by pressure not pleasure, the one who dislikes exercise, the people-pleaser, and the persecuted. All of these identities and ways of being are no longer sustainable. Sorry, no room. Use by date hit. Expired. See you later.

How about you?

What is falling away? What wants to uproot? What part of you is becoming harder to tie down? What is becoming less and less important? How is Life trying to change you? What is ready to move on? What is moving away from you? What do you find draining to hold on to? What used to be important to you but now is not so much? If you weren't afraid of nothing coming to take its place, what would you release?

RISE SISTER RISE

What is falling away?

What ways of being are no longer sustainable?

What identities are you ready to let go of?

How does your life need to change in order
to accommodate letting this/these go?

△

While it served her in the past
She refused to keep her magic
contained, restrained,
or detained any longer.

GRANDMOTHER MOON

May we loosen our grip and open our hearts.

May we release all that is no longer a vibrational match.

May our hearts be open, stretched, and full.

May our arms and minds stay open so that
what is on its way can arrive swiftly.

May our mouths be used as vehicles of truth, integrity, and peace.

May our creations travel, our new projects be ignited,
our deepest prayers be heard, and our hearts held
by the mysterious force that simply is.

And so it is, and so it is, and so it is.

Part III

REMEMBERING OUR CYCLIC NATURE

She was one with the Earth
And the Earth was one with Her.

△

YOU ARE SPIRIT EARTHED

Your purpose is to be spirit embodied. To ground your awakened consciousness in the third dimension. Earth is a sacred ecosystem that is not just our home, but also something we are very much a part of. Every time we resist our true nature, doubt our intuition, give away our power, question our worth, or contain what is rising in us, we fall out of flow with Life.

Billions of years have come before you and billions will follow. You decided to be here right now. In this moment of significant change. In this moment of upheaval. In this moment of great potential to create significant shifts in consciousness. In this Age of Light. There is no coincidence that you are here.

Everything we do to the Earth we do to ourselves, as a species we have disconnected from our Mother. Fallen out of her natural rhythmic cycles and flow. Mother Earth doesn't need us in order to survive but we need Her.

What happens in one happens to the whole.

When one of us surrenders to our true nature it becomes easier for others to surrender to theirs.

No matter where
She was in the world,
She always found Her
true nature in nature.

△

YOU'LL FIND YOUR TRUE
NATURE IN NATURE

'You will find something more in woods than books.
Trees and stones will teach you that which
you can never learn from masters.'
SAINT BERNARD

I grew up in Australia by the ocean. The cars on my street would rust quickly in the salty air. And looking back I see how the sea breeze cleansed, released and regenerated so much for me too. My feet would be in the sand pretty much every day. If not, then the rocks or grass. Nature was a huge part of my life, but I didn't think anything of it.

When I moved to London my whole body mourned the loss of the saltwater. I started craving it like a drug. I'd pile bucketloads of sea salt into my bath and onto my food. But it wasn't the salt that I was missing, as much as the presence of the wild element itself. On my skin, messing up my hair, Her waves churning through my limbs. But my busy life didn't allow the time to ponder over what it was that made my heart feel like it was ever so slowly closing up.

When my life fell apart in 2011, I remember being on the floor of my apartment, which had just begun to flood. I had just burst into tears and the water pipes burst in unison. The water was my message that the way I was living could not go on. While I was on my knees I prayed for guidance. I knew something had to change. Tuning in to my intuition, I was led to follow what lit me up and it brought me back to nature. And indeed my own true nature.

I discovered London parks, rose gardens, and wisdom keepers in the shape of trees. As I allowed myself to be at one with nature, I felt myself coming back to life. As I allowed myself to truly see the nature around me, I started seeing myself mirrored back. As I allowed myself to be led by nature, I reconnected back to my inner compass. As I allowed myself to notice and listen to nature, I began hearing the whispers of my soul. As I allowed myself to be held by nature, I found myself being held by all of Life.

No matter how disconnected, confused, lost, broken, betrayed, or hurt you find yourself, you can find your true nature in nature.

Nature is a living, breathing mirror of who we are. We see ourselves as separate from it but in fact we are part of it. Nature is teaching us how to be human every moment of every day. The rose coaxes us to open and soften our heart. The oak teaches us to drop our roots deep in order to stand tall. The sand assures us that change is inevitable and that we are always altering in form. The frangipani reminds us of the sweetness of life. The shell whispers secrets long forgotten. The butterfly proves that there is life after loss. The volcano tells us that if we hold it in, eventually we will explode. No matter who you are, you will find your true nature in nature.

There is wisdom in the plants and trees and rocks and the Earth below us but we cannot unlock it if we don't connect and listen. Mother Earth is constantly whispering, waiting for us to connect with her secrets. The ancients knew this. It's time for us all to remember.

When you connect with nature you are connecting with all of Life – the everything of every possible moment. If you make connecting to nature part of your daily practice, you will awaken your senses enough to notice the subtle changes in your life. If you focus on how it feels to be in nature – the earth beneath your feet, the scent in the air, the sun on your face, the water on your skin, the flowers opening for you in all their glory – you will be activating your feeling body. When your feeling body is activated your soul is able to be grounded in your body. It is in this place that your soul's whispers can be heard most clearly and divine ideas can land on your lap.

Nature is always present, it's we who are not. When you take a moment to *be* truly in nature, you discover how many gifts She offers you every moment of every day.

PRACTICE: INTUITIVE NATURE WALKING

My favorite tool for increasing your intuition and getting into the flow of Life is to spend time in nature doing a practice I call 'Intuitive Nature Walking.' All you need to do is find a large part of nature – ideally a park, a beach, forest, or bushland and allow yourself to be moved by the Shakti of Life.

Walk and be moved with no attachment to the outcome.

If you feel yourself being led to a big tree then walk to the big tree. If you find yourself being led to lie on the earth, lie on the earth. If you feel guided to climb a rock, climb a rock.

Notice the beauty around you. Allow nature to move you. Trust the process as you allow nature to intuitively guide you home.

RISE SISTER RISE

Take yourself on an Intuitive Nature Walk. Go into nature, set your alarm for 20 minutes and allow yourself to be moved by the Shakti of Life.

△

The paper bark from her childhood
whispered tales of the cyclic
nature of letting go.

Its message had remained constant
three and a third decades on.

But it took her to circle the Earth
more times than she had fingers before
She was finally able to hear it.

△

WHEN WHISPERS TURN INTO SHOUTS

Why do we feel the need to conquer nature? To own it. To bend it to our will. We see ourselves as civilized. But it is not civilized to destroy your own habitat. It's not civilized to destroy the very things that you are dependent on to breathe, drink, and eat. It is not civilized to neglect the weak and the poor. It is not civilized to bring harm to your species. What happened to our human nature? We see ourselves as separate from nature but we are not. We see ourselves as separate from the Earth, as living on it, but our bodies are the Earth itself.

We attempt to own this planet and every plot of land. But it has never been ours to claim. If we don't stop soon, we'll be another ancient land sunken and forgotten. I don't know about you but I'm too tired to do it all again. Let's learn from the ancients. From their wisdom and their mistakes.

Everything we do to the Earth, we are really doing to ourselves. When we see a tree being chopped down, let's see a friend. When we throw our trash in the dump, let's see it in our home. I believe we can turn this around. It is still possible for us to create heaven on Earth.

RISE SISTER RISE

How is Mother Earth whispering to you? How
is She guiding you to act on Her behalf?

△

WHISPERS FROM MOTHER EARTH

Mother Earth is always whispering. Telling you secrets of times past and guiding you every moment of every day. If you're ever stuck, go out and let Her welcome you into Her arms. She has so much to tell you and can soothe you in no time at all.

PRACTICE: WHISPERS FROM MOTHER EARTH

Put your phone on 'do not disturb', be truly present in the moment, and connect with Mother Earth.

Go to your favorite park, sit under your favorite tree, climb your favorite mountain, walk along your favorite beach. Ask Mother Earth to speak to you and get ready to capture her whispers. You may want to ask her a question or you could keep it open.

Breathe deeply and allow yourself to hear her whispers deep in your heart, capturing her words of wisdom on your phone or in a notebook. You may receive them one word at a time or it may be a feeling you have.

Imagine each one being a golden thread that you're pulling ever so softly. Share your whispers from Mother Earth by posting it to Instagram using the hash tags #WhispersFromMotherEarth and #RiseSisterRise

$\triangle$

YOUR RELATIONSHIP WITH THE SEASONS

The earth is sentient. As it breathes in and out the whole planet does too. It has its own heartbeat, its own natural rhythm in the form of seasons. As the trees release their leaves, we are prompted to let go too.

The way the modern world has developed has resulted in so many of us becoming disconnected from the subtle shifts in rhythm that the seasons bring, disconnecting ourselves little by little from the heartbeat of the planet and thus the flow of Life. So many of us spend our days in brightly lit offices with the temperature set all year round. Our bodies missing out on their daily dose of natural light and the balancing touch of raw earth beneath our feet.

Don't overlook the powerful effect seasonal awareness and the Earth's touch has in bringing your body back to flow. Nature and its seasons are waiting at the ready to bring us back into harmony with ourselves, the Earth and the Universe at large.

I had been living in the UK for almost 10 years when I finally understood the importance of seasons and the necessity of winter. Born in spring, I am a warm-weather woman. Each December, as the holiday lights were being switched on, you would find me dragging an oversized suitcase to the nearest airport, boycotting winter and escaping somewhere sunny.

But by sidestepping winter, my body didn't receive the gifts of rest and rejuvenation that the darker months bring. My inner fire wasn't being stoked. By the time spring came along, I lacked the clarity and newfound energy that it brings. Without the abundant reserves needed to go out into the world again, my body fell into a deep exhaustion and I would have to reach for caffeine to keep me going. I would blame it on too much holiday cheer or jetlag, but eventually I realized that my inner seasons were crying out for attention.

In a 10-year period, there was one year that I stayed and let winter work Her magic. A year earlier I had broken up with my long-term partner and he had moved back to Australia. Knowing that being in the same country wouldn't be beneficial, I bunkered up in my Notting Hill studio apartment for a long and lonely winter. To make matters worse, all of my friends had left the city, leaving me pretty much alone for the holidays. The days were dark, the nights long and cold. I barely left home except to arm myself with a gourmet pizza from the local Italian, some dark chocolate, and a bottle of Cab Sauv. It was the worst and best period of my life.

During these dark days and evenings, bunkered up in a blanket and thermals, I was able to fully hit my rock bottom. And it was here that I found myself. In those weeks, when it felt like the whole city had gone into hibernation, I fanned the flames of my inner light and finally committed to quitting my job, following my passion, and starting a new life for myself. Had I not let the darkness and bitter winds of my inner winter be realized, perhaps I wouldn't have found the potent clarity that that winter gave me.

Develop a relationship with the changing seasons around you. Notice the hope and inspiration of spring, the celebration, rising and outward connection of summer, the falling away and letting go of fall (autumn), and the replenishment, clarity, rest, surrendering, and potency of winter.

RISE SISTER RISE

List the seasons in your order of preference.

Look at your least favorite season and ask
yourself: What gifts does this season have for me
that my body and soul are yearning for?

△

HONORING YOUR INNER RHYTHM

When you are here on a mission and you hear the call from spirit to change things, it is easy to fall into endurance mode. I have done it time and time again. Put being of service ahead of my own body's needs. This must stop. If we are to do the work of change, we must be sustainable.

If we are pushing or striving, we are out of flow with the natural rhythm of the planet. If we are out of flow with the Earth, we not only make it harder for ourselves but also put stress on the planet. We must stop pushing and pressuring ourselves. We are here to do a life's work, not a season. Do not burn out now. You are needed for the long haul. It is time that we deeply honor these cycles, and stop expecting things and ourselves to be always on (in summer mode).

If you push yourself to be always producing, your creative well will soon run dry. You cannot possibly create the potency of the work that you are here to create, if you are trying to bloom. Do not let what others are doing pressure you into more doing. You only have to keep up with the world around you if you are choosing to compete in the first place.

There is a perfect time for everything. If the tulip surfaces in the heart of winter the bitter winds won't give her a chance. She will lose her supple petals and be bitten by unforgiving frost. If she attempts to endure on through to the end of summer she will become parched and dry up.

If the cherry blossom got impatient and pushed herself to bloom because the daffodils were out, we would miss that magical moment where all of a sudden, her soft subtle scent fills the balmy twilight air.

Trust the natural flow of your inner seasons and don't push yourself to bloom all year round. There are times for sowing, times for blossoming, and times for retreating and going into hibernation. There is plenty of room for all of us to rise in our own perfect time.

What is another person's summer may be your winter. But come spring, positions will be reversed. Trust your inner seasons and remember: spring returns to delight us each and every year.

#RISESISTERRISE MANTRA

I honor my inner seasons and deeply trust my inner rhythm. There is no rush. In perfect time I rise.

RISE SISTER RISE

Are you respecting the seasons of your life or are you attempting to bloom all year round?

Δ

THE MYSTERY OF SHE

Her heart was connected to the flowers.

As they opened, so did She.

Her voice was connected to the birds.

As they sang, so did She.

Her wisdom was connected to the trees.

As they whispered, so did She.

Her womb was connected to the moon.

As it waxed and waned, so did She.

Her attachments were connected to the tides.

As they let go, so did She.

Her passions were connected to the fire.

As it was stoked, so was She.

Her eyes were connected to the entire sky.

As it saw clearly, so did She.

Her emotions were connected to the rivers.

As they flowed, so did She.

Her spirit was connected to the stars.

As they shone, so did She.

Her soul was connected to the entire Universe.

As it expanded, so did She.

△

YOUR MONTHLY CYCLE AS YOUR TEACHER

'The womb is not a place to store fear and pain. The womb is a place to create and give birth to life'

13TH RITE OF THE MUNAY-KI, *THE RITE OF THE WOMB*

Some women don't have any problems when it comes to period pain. I am not one of them. Ever since I was 14 my periods caused me agony. Most months would find me curled up in the fetal position. Debilitated by the excruciating daggers, cramps and deep aches coming from my uterus. I would wake up some mornings feeling like I was being ripped open from within. Having to call up work and make some excuse for why I couldn't come in. There was no way I was using my womanhood as an excuse – that would be admitting weakness, or so I thought back then.

Someone who prided herself on having a high pain threshold, I just accepted the pain (endometriosis) as a part of life that I would need to endure and suck up. Part and parcel of being a woman. Had I experienced the same pain while not having my period, I would have run myself straight to the hospital every month.

For someone so conscious this was extremely out of character. For all other ailments you'd find me inquiring into my body – seeing a kinesiologist, changing my diet, doing EFT (emotional freedom technique). You name it, I'd try it. Anything to learn the lesson and free myself from pain. But when it came to my womb, it was as if some part of me was saying, *'This is your lot, this is what you have to endure because you are a woman.'* And so for four days every month my body went into survival mode. I pushed it down and silenced the moans that my body longed to make. With every new year the pain got fiercer, my womb making more and more of an effort to get my attention. It took almost 20 years of increased monthly agony for me to allow myself finally to listen to what She was trying to tell me.

Period pain is our womb talking to us. The feminine trying to get our attention. It's linked to our lineage, both family and soul, so many of us are carrying pain and fear from times past – ours and that of those who came before us (ancestral line). Unexpressed anger, rage and remembering of times where stuff happened to women and our bodies that just was not right. In my work I have found that many of the women who are here to do the work of the rising feminine suffer greatly with menstruation. It's time that we heal the pain, shame, and suffering carried in the collective female consciousness.

My cycle has been such a rich teacher and self-development tool. The thought that I ignored it for so long saddens me. The fact that we don't learn this stuff in school makes me angry. The fact that so many of us hold shame and disgust about something that is such a normal thing and a potent guide baffles me. The female cycle should be celebrated, not hushed and kept hidden. When we tap into the flow of our body's cycles, we enter into a magnificent dance with all of life.

My CEO from my first job out of university was a serious powerhouse. One of the few women right up the top of the ladder in the industry and my first corporate female role model. One evening she found me keeled over by the pain of my period. I was horrified that she had caught me, until she confessed that she suffered in the same way. She said that acupuncture and Chinese medicine helped some, but even still she had to turn down some serious jobs because she knew she wouldn't be on her game for five days each month.

We shared a moment of deep sisterhood that day and a joint pain of the cost of a patriarchal corporate system that didn't honor the cyclic nature of our bodies.

In ancient times, when women had their period, they would retreat from the rest of the village into a Red Tent while they bled. It was thought that when women bled they were at their most potent and closest to the Goddess. Most women bled in sync so this was a time when women would rest, connect, rejuvenate, heal, let go, and bleed on behalf of the community. Stories would be shared and a sacred sisterhood formed. I believe that at root level, this is something that women of our era deeply yearn for without realizing. It is through the sharing of stories that wisdom is passed down and we connect with our fellow sisters as We, not She vs. Me.

The rise of female entrepreneurs running online businesses from home and corporations offering remote working is a great step in the direction of giving us the freedom to honor our bodies and prioritize our wellbeing. However as women who have worked in the corporate world, we need to be careful that we don't just take the existing patriarchal corporate models and enforce them in our home-based businesses too. We need to create new models of working that honor the cyclic nature of our bodies.

I now don't book client sessions, interviews, or meetings on the days that I am bleeding, in the knowledge that this is when my wisdom is most potent (*see page 118* for more on this). On these days I bunker up ready to receive the blueprint for the month ahead: concise clarity on decisions I need to make, and ready to receive downloads in full.

So many women hold unexpressed emotions such as fear, pain, anger, and grief in their womb. Often it's not even ours, rather something we have inherited, passed down to us through our ancestral lines from earlier times. When women had no choice but to contain our sexuality, power, wisdom, rage, and voice. When our bodies were not our own. When our Shakti was taken rather than honored.

Many women I know, who are doing the work of the feminine, have had their wombs talk to them through physical period pain, endometriosis, polycystic ovaries or other dis-ease. It's as if they are carrying the pain and suffering of not only their lineage but of all women too.

The thing that spurred the healing of my female cycle was receiving the 13th rite of the Munay-Ki: The Rite of the Womb. This rite was passed down to shaman Marcela Lobos in 2014 from the women of a Peruvian tribe called the Munay-Ki – a lineage which has freed itself from suffering. These women want all of us to remember:

'The womb is not a place to store fear and pain.

The womb is a place to create and give birth to life.'

Once a woman has received the rite she is encouraged to share it with other women. If you would like to find out more about receiving the Rite of the Womb, go to www.riteofthewomb.com or if you attend a Rise Sister Rise workshop or retreat, come up and ask to receive it.

RISE SISTER RISE

What is your relationship with your period?

What is your womb trying to tell you?

If you experience pain, whose pain is it that you are holding?

What is your womb trying to free you from?

△

THE FOUR STAGES OF
WOMANHOOD AND UNLOCKING
THE POWER OF YOUR PERIOD

'I bleed every month and do not die. How am I not magic?'
NAYYIRAH WAHEED

The Maiden, the Mother, the Wild and Wise Woman, and the Crone signify the four main stages that women journey through over the duration of our lives.

These periods of transition are generally marked by four significant life-changing events: menstruation; sex or marriage (or partnership); childbirth; and menopause. In ancient times, they were also marked with ceremony and ritual that ushered in each new life stage. That is, women were initiated into each stage of womanhood. Today these transitions are rarely honored in a sacred way, and thus many of us fall short of transitioning fully into our womanhood. This period of history needs fierce women in their power, who have crossed the threshold from girlhood and been initiated into womanhood.

Our menstrual cycle is connected to the phases of the moon and, as the moon waxes and wanes, our bodies also transition through the four archetypes of womanhood each and every month. As the moon controls our cycles, the more attention we put on harmonizing our monthly cycles, the more in sync with the Universe we become, and the more in sync with all of Life we feel.

Journeying through each stage of womanhood each month can feel as if we are having the rug pulled out from underneath us. In a way we are. But if we begin to see this process as an invitation to reclaim all aspects of who we are as a woman each month, everything changes. Your period then becomes a monthly initiation in deepening your potency as a wise, creative, powerful woman. Before I began working on my cycle I felt like a crazy woman every month. One moment I would be happy and excited about the future, the next I'd be sensitive and wanting to hide from the world. One week I'd be caring and encouraging and the next I'd be wanting to burn everything down. Tuning in to the significant, subtle changes our cycle takes us in every month, and how each of these stages relates to the different archetypes of being a woman, the whole thing makes so much more sense (and you feel a lot less crazy).

Working with your cycle you will be able to awaken the untapped power that perhaps you didn't know you had and be able to tune in to the fierce feminine wisdom that all women have access to.

Here are the four main female stages of womanhood and how they relate to our monthly cycles.

1. The Maiden (pre-ovulation)

The Maiden is young, enthusiastic, strong, independent, determined, excitable, hopeful, courageous, energized, boundless, and positive. Full of ideas and excited about the future, what she lacks in years, she makes up in enthusiasm and zest for life. The Maiden is the Virgin, the innocent part of us that sees potential in everything. She is a woman one-in-herself. She sees the magic in everything.

Shadow Maiden: Naive, self-centered, impressionable, inexperienced, lacking confidence, too many ideas, spends lots of time in thought, good at starting things but lacks drive to finish them, full of hope and big ideas but easily discouraged as they are not fully grounded yet; a tendency to overcommit, she says yes because she gets overexcited or doesn't want to miss out

Season: Spring (full of possibility)

Element: Air

Moon phase: Waxing/New moon

Rite of passage: Menarche (getting your period, becoming a woman)

Idols: Brighid, Athena, Priestess, Ostara, Persephone

Notes for Rising
This is the time for coming up with lots of ideas, playing and dreaming about what could be without restriction. Write your dreams, make your plans, the sky is the limit.

2. The Mother (ovulation)

The Mother is the fertile part of us, the part of us that births things into the world for real. She is compassionate, protective, nurturing, devotional, understanding, encouraging, and big-hearted. She is loving and nurturing, but also committed to doing whatever it takes to get the job done. She is able to take the energy and enthusiasm of the Maiden and turn it into focused action. Able to birth both life and creations into the world. Manifesting thought and concept into form.

Shadow Mother: Overprotective, smothering, forgetting to look after self, controlling, codependence, abandoning, exhaustion, doesn't know when to stop, making others feel guilty for not needing her

Season: Summer (everything is fertile)

Element: Fire

Moon phase: Full moon

Rites of passage: Marriage (or partnership) and birth (both life and more metaphorically e.g. birthing a creation)

Idols: Isis, Gaia, Mother Mary, Hathor, Quan Yin, Amma, Demeter, Rhea

Notes for Rising
You're likely to feel and look at your best here. This is the ideal time to commit to what is rising in you and go about making it happen for real. Launch the program, write the book, host the event.

3. The Wise, Wild Woman (premenstrual)

The Wise, Wild Woman is uninhibited and wise. She has journeyed through Maidenhood and Motherhood, knows who she is and isn't afraid to show it. Also known as the Medicine Woman or the Healer, she is in touch with and recognized for her inner medicine and magic. She knows her worth, is guided by her intuition and calls upon it regularly.

There is a certain ruthlessness about her because she can see through what is important and what isn't. You can't pull the wool over her eyes, she knows her power and she demands your respect. If you push her or do not respect her she will react and it might not be pretty. She's fierce. She's not afraid of what people think. She's not afraid to do what it takes to get what she wants.

Shadow Wild Woman: Crazy, ruthless, angry, jealous, vindictive, impatient, blunt, end justifies the means

Season: Fall/autumn (things are falling away)

Element: Water

Moon phase: Waning moon

Rites of passage: Significant loss or mourning, such as death, loss of job, separation, an emotional ending, children leaving home; Saturn returns, being initiated by a mentor or teacher

Idols: Artemis, The Wolf, Kali, Tara, Saraswati, witch, healer, medicine woman

Notes for Rising

This is the best place to let things go, to refine, perfect, and refocus. Dance, sing, or do whatever you can to express and transmute your feelings into passion. It's a great time to de-clutter your life, negotiate fiercely, protect your boundaries, and create powerful and authentic work.

4. The Crone (menstruation)

In ancient societies the Crone was highly revered, however today she is often not given the reverence she deserves. She is the wisdom keeper, the one who has the ultimate perspective and has nothing left to prove. She is able to see with absolute clarity and advise in a selfless way, as she has no ulterior motives. She has a certain patience about her, having been through it all herself, and no longer cares what people think.

The Crone is the part of us that is most potent in her wisdom. Is able to see through all inauthenticity and patterns from afar. While the Maiden has an innocent purity about her, the Crone has a certain purity as well. She is closest to Source and in surrender to Life.

Shadow Crone: Brutal, hermit, crazy, unforgiving, judgmental, bitter, jaded, lonely, self-pitying, defeated

Period cycle: Menstruation

Season: Winter

Element: Earth

Moon phase: Dark/New moon

Rite of passage: Menopause

Idols: Vali Myers, Maya Angelou, Woman of the Mist, Baba Yaga, Fairy Godmother, Morrigan, Cerridwen, Hecate

Notes for Rising

This is the best part of your cycle during which to rest. Don't believe you need to be physically active to be productive. It's an amazing time to make a decision, get clarity on a future project or be with the energy of what is rising in you. Prior to working with my cycle, I dreaded the premenstrual (Wise, Wild Woman – fall/autumn) and menstruation (Crone – winter) parts of my cycle. I was much more comfortable in the pre-ovulation (Maiden – spring) and ovulation (Mother – summer).

However, after working with my cycle, I discovered that it was actually in fall/autumn (premenstrual) and winter (menstruation) that my hidden power lay. When I began honoring my body and listening to her pain during these times rather than numb or push on through, I was able to unlock a potent power within me that I now channel into my work. Even better, I was able to heal ancient patriarchal wounds around the shame of being a woman and reduce my period pain tenfold. I cannot believe I am saying this, but I now look forward to having my period.

If you have any problems or pains with your menstrual cycle, I so recommend that you continue this work in more depth. In doing so you will discover a deeper relationship to yourself, a compassion for your body, connection with the Earth, and to all women. I recommend the work of Lisa Lister and Alexandra Pope if you feel called to work with your female cycle.

RISE SISTER RISE

What is your relationship with your monthly cycle?
Do you currently track it? Are you in tune with
it? Do you feel as though the rug is being pulled
from underneath you on a regular basis?

Which part of your monthly cycle do you enjoy the
most – pre-ovulation (spring), ovulation (summer),
premenstrual (fall/autumn), menstruation (winter)?

Which part of your monthly cycle do you struggle with
the most – pre-ovulation (spring), ovulation (summer),
premenstrual (autumn), menstruation (winter)?

What is your body yearning for at these
times that you are not giving it?

What is the untapped power that this stage of
your cycle might hold for you if you listened to
your body and gave it what it needed?

△

BEING HUMAN IS HARD

No one is immune to life's pleasures and pains. Earth is a planet of polarity and sometimes being human is HARD! The pleasures stretch our heart and the pains do exactly the same thing. We are here to grow through the pleasures and the pains. We cannot use spirituality to avoid the pains or to hold on to the pleasures forever. Oh cyclic nature of life, you get us every time.

The more time you have spent in spirit form, the more difficult you may find being in a human body. Many of us have incarnated on other planets where third-dimensional laws just don't exist. This is one reason why we may feel so heavy, uncomfortable and trapped in our physical bodies, using food and other substances to check out or keep ourselves grounded.

So many of our souls are not anchored in our bodies. When we have our spiritual awakening, many get lost in the higher chakras, flying off into the cosmos remembering that we are spirit. However, we must not forget that we chose to be here right now, to have this human experience, and so our purpose is to ground those spiritual energies in human form.

There are so many delights that this planet has to offer. Sex, falling in love, chocolate, the sheer beauty of roses, the pleasure of gravity as you jump off a rock into crystal-clear salt water, lying on hot sand and being held by Mother Earth, the magnificent design and taste of strawberries, raspberries and passion fruit (oh God passion fruit – if that was man-made we would be in utter awe).

The delights are endless and absolutely awe-worthy when you take a moment to truly taste, smell, hear, and see the beautiful wonder of planet Earth. It is easy to get lost in the pain and suffering that happens here, however, we must do our best not to busy ourselves too much that we miss the bountiful pleasures that She is serving us every moment of every day. Seek them and your spirit will be delighted to be grounded.

Sometimes when we experience great sadness or tragedy, it may cause a soul to want to leave the body. The best way to call it back is to lose yourself in the sheer delights of being human. To let nature coax you back into your body. To feel the sand beneath your toes. The sun on your skin. The taste of cacao melting on your tongue.

Bring yourself back into the pleasures of being human by slowing down and noticing the beauty that is surrounding you now.

RISE SISTER RISE

Buy yourself a passion fruit. Set aside a couple of minutes to look at it deeply, smell its fragrance, admire its color and intricate design. Slowly taste its nectar, as you receive the sweetness and exoticness that this planet has to offer you in every single moment. Take in the pleasure of being human.

△

IT'S YOUR HUMANNESS
THAT INSPIRES ME

It is your humanness that inspires me:

Your ability to choose to rise, fall after fall.

It's your humanness that inspires me:

The time you chose the light when it was darker than ever before.

It's your humanness that inspires me:

How you found the courage to let the life you had
so consciously created crumble and fall.

It's your humanness that inspires me:

When you share your heart, cracks and all.

It's your humanness that inspires me:

That you tell the truth about how hard life got
and how you're different from before.

It's your humanness that inspires me:

The day you let your old self die, in order for
who you were becoming to be born.

It's your humanness that inspires me:

How no matter how many times you doubted it,
You never stopped answering the call.

△

PRAY INTO THE ANXIETY

Two years ago I woke up with this subtle yet uncomfortable anxious feeling. I couldn't remember how long it had been there or when it started. The truth is, I don't remember ever not feeling it.

The reason it felt foreign is because I had never actually allowed myself to feel it in full. The moment it came up I'd push it back down in an effort to stop feeling it. So many of us live our lives like this, with subtle undercurrents of emotion that we're not aware of.

I spent months trying to do all that I could to shake it using every single tool in my kit. Frustrated that nothing I tried could ever quite free me from its presence, I finally surrendered. Instead of pushing it away, I allowed it to be fully here.

I realized how I had been looking at this anxiety as a feeling that needed to be fixed. Something that should go away. Something that I should not be feeling.

I realized how I had seen my negative emotions, pain, and suffering as things that I needed to overcome. Things I should be ashamed of feeling. Where the truth is that all feelings and parts of the human experience are holy.

So each time I noticed the feeling return, instead of pushing it into the shadows (where it could control me), or trying to fix it, I would invite it in fully.

By allowing my anxiety to come sit beside me the prayer energy was finally able to reach it, to envelop it, to cradle it, to soften it. Shakti was free to do Her thing.

Instead of being held. Stuck. Stagnant. I began to notice each time it sparked up throughout my day. In each moment I'd allow myself to feel it fully.

By allowing it all to be here, I saw how this anxiety had actually been a powerful driving force in me getting stuff done. A superpower of sorts, scaring me into being productive. Could I still be successful without this pressure as my driver?

RISE SISTER RISE

The feelings that you banish are the path to your peace and the secret to unleashing your unstoppable power. Start to become aware of the undercurrent feelings that you push away. It is the subtle ones that are in the driver's seat of your life. Invite them to step forward and be fully present, rather than casting them aside to the dungeon where they secretly hold the keys.

Breathe in and out deeply and inquire, do you have an undercurrent emotion that you just can't shake? If you had to give it a name, what would it be – anxious, fear of being caught out, not good enough, etc.? Name your undercurrent emotion now.

Instead of pushing it aside, allow it to be completely here now and invite the prayer energy to reach it, offering it up as you do. Continue to do this every time you notice this undercurrent emotion begin to rise.

PLEASURE NOT PRESSURE

We are either driven by pressure or driven by pleasure. The amount of work we do is the same. Choose pleasure not pressure.

As I described previously, my undercurrent driving force when I worked in advertising was pressure (*see page 11*). So why did I find myself years later living the life I deeply desired, doing what brought me pleasure, while still having pressure as my driving force? It's because while I changed my life, I didn't change the old system. I was using the old patriarchal model in the new life I had created for myself. It was like I had the latest MacBook Air with an operating system from the 1990s.

So many of us have learned to use fear as our driver. To be motivated by what we want to avoid, rather than what we would be delighted to create. We are in survival mode, not trusting life or anything around us. So attached to outcomes that we strive to get the job and then, once we have it, we either put on extra pressure to get the next thing or to ensure that we don't lose what we have. In doing so we deny ourselves the pleasure of actually enjoying the very thing we worked so hard to create.

When you make pleasure your driving force, the doing is a joy and the outcome is irrelevant. When you make pressure your driving force, the doing is a stress and the outcome is always changing. It is irrelevant what you are doing, what is relevant is the undercurrent emotion that is driving it. You can change your entire life, but if you don't update the system nothing will really change.

Take writing this book for example. I could sit down and be driven by the pressure of:

Will my readers like it, will my publisher like it, will it be the worst book ever written in all of human history, will it sell as many copies as my first, when should I write the next one, what if it has been written before, what if I don't get it done in time, what if I have to rewrite it completely, what if I am not exercising enough, what if I am not spending enough time with my family and friends?

OR...

I could be driven by the pleasure of actually writing it:

I can't believe that I get to spend my time sharing my heart, that I can freely share my voice. I just love being able to write on a Sunday while it's raining outside and I am wearing the cashmere socks I got for Christmas. How great is it that I can have a dance break in the middle of my home 'office.' I just love letting nature inspire me and sharing her whispers, I love writing so much and love that I have managed to create a life that lets me do just that, how lucky am I?

The action is exactly the same, the end point is too; however, the enjoyment levels are polar opposites.

When you make pressure your driving force, each decision is based on what you want to avoid rather than what you will enjoy.

#RISESISTERRISE MANTRA

Pleasure not pressure.

RISE SISTER RISE

Are you driven by pleasure or pressure?

How can you make pleasure your driving force?

△

MOTHER EARTH IS BUSY WEAVING THE THREADS OF YOUR LIFE

You don't need to be busy for things to be happening. If you're someone who gets lit up by self-improvement this one is extra important. If you're doing all the time, there's not space for Mother Earth to do anything for you.

Put time aside for unattached nothingness. Creating, playing, and relaxing. Not for the outcome of where it will get you or what it will give you, but for the pure pleasure of it. Don't fall back into the patriarchal linear thinking that in order to be productive you need to be active at all times. When you play or commune with nature you fall back into flow with Life. Mother Earth is busy knitting the tapestry of your life when you least expect it. Instead of relying on your masculine reserves of endurance, work at fine-tuning your intuition and move when you are called to move.

The Universe is always hard at work for you, serving you. Every step you take toward the flow of Life, Life takes three.

RISE SISTER RISE

Do you believe you need to be busy in order to be productive? What could you delegate to Mother Earth while you spend some time relaxing? Put in your requests.

PRACTICE: A LETTER TO MY DAUGHTER

Write a letter to yourself from the Great Mother. What does She want you to know? What does She want you to remember?

△

HELD

The Mother is waiting to hold you. To support you. To show you the way. To guide your each and every move. But in order for Her to do so, you need to be willing to be held. Like really held. Totally. In full. 100 percent. Held. If you only allow 50 percent that's how much support you will receive. However unmet you feel by Life, that's the amount you are resisting being held.

Being held takes courage. It takes faith. For it requires that you allow all control, scheming, and relying on your own strength to dissolve away.

The next time you feel fearful or like you are resisting Life, try my Held practice below. It works every time.

PRACTICE: BEING HELD

If you have grass or nature near you do this in nature. If not, lie down on a bed or on the floor.

Start to slow your breathing and notice the earth (ground/bed) beneath you. Notice how it feels on your back, bottom, feet, legs, neck, shoulders, head.

Notice how relaxed or tense your body is. How much you are relying on your own strength, your muscles to hold you up. Notice how tight or relaxed they are. Just notice.

Breathing in really deeply hold your breath and squeeeeeeeeeeze every single muscle in your body. Hold your breath for eight seconds... And let go...

As you release your breath, release every single ounce of resistance in your body allowing the Earth to hold you in full.

Feel yourself getting heavier as you let go of control. Melt into the Earth. Feel Her pulse. Allow the Mother to hold you in full.

See if you can feel the pulse of the Earth as She breathes in and out – breathe with Her. Let Her breathe you. Drink in Her nectar. Let Her cradle you back home to you.

RISE SISTER RISE

Do the above exercise in bed as soon as you wake up in the morning and before you go to sleep. As you are doing it affirm: 'I am willing to be held in full by the Mother and all of Life.'

Δ

She never walked alone.

For She was ever held by She.

△

LEADING FROM THE FEMININE

'Woman has to understand her role. Her role is not to worship God; Her role is to be the very self of God. Her oneness can affect and open every heart.'

Yogi Bhajan

To lead in this new age we can't rely on our masculine reserves, or expect others to do the same just because we had to in our time. If we want to bring about a significant shift on the planet we must replace all-nighters with early-morning *sadhana*, fear with compassion, and stress with surrender.

This era of slogging it out has got to stop. When we push on through we are relying on our own strength; when we are relying on our own strength we are operating from our separate selves. When we are operating form our separate selves, we are resisting being in flow with the universal flow of Life. When we resist the Universal flow of Life, life is hard.

As women we are creators. Always giving birth to something new. The creative process is just that: A process. Filled with periods of time when you generate ideas, periods when you walk away from it, periods when you peel back the layers, periods when you want to throw in the towel, and periods when you share it to the world. In order for the juices to keep flowing, we must respect the ebbs and flows of doing, receiving and letting it be.

As I shared in an earlier chapter (*see page 24*) when my work started taking off, I found there weren't enough hours in the day. I was reaching overwhelm and exhaustion at a rapid rate. Yet the fear of stopping and potentially missing out on opportunities that might never come back drove me to keep pushing on, enduring, thinking that it would eventually slow down. Six months in, there were no signs of that happening at all. Picking up on my rapidly approaching exhaustion, my intuition told me I needed to do three things, if I was going to create a life's work not a season:

1. Halve my working hours.

2. Double my devotion.

3. Prioritize my personal life.

Now, at the time the part of me who prided herself on working hard and always pushing on through went into a panic. *Who would I be without this identity?* I used to blame the industry I was in (advertising) for my tendency to overwork. But there I was years later, overworked and exhausted. The common link was me.

I finally surrendered to the truth that I couldn't keep going that way, reduced my hours and replaced the time with a cocktail of prayer and play instead. The less I worked, the more I actually got done. Time got stretchy.

The less time I had, the easier it was to say no. The more I said no, the more energy I had. The more energy I had, the more productive I was. The more productive I was, the more fulfilled I felt. The more I increased my devotion, the more support I received from the world around me. The more I played, the more aha moments I had and the more excited I got about showing up to work.

RISE SISTER RISE

How are you being called to lead from
a more feminine perspective?

△

A LIFE'S WORK, NOT A SEASON

Be committed to creating a life's work, not a season. If you get overexcited and rush everything for fear of missing out, you run the risk of being a flash in the pan and fading away fast. Have the stamina to stay in the game. To do it for the devotion and pleasure alone. Create your art for life and your life for your art. Withstand the winds of time. Sustain the changing trends. Leave a legacy.

Respect the work of those who have come before you by creating you own unique thing. Create what you came here to create, not an appropriation of what others have already done. Drink deep from your roots of congruency. These are what will hold you through the seasons of your life.

Don't rush the process. Allow your fruits of originality to ripen in their own sweet time, knowing there will always be plenty more where they came from. Don't push yourself and dry out. Tend to your garden so that it is always fertile, so that you have new unique creations grow in your gardens each and every year. There is no race. There is no competition. Go steady and flourish. Commit to creating a life's work, not a season.

RISE SISTER RISE

What needs to happen for you to create
a life's work, not a season?

△

FILLING UP YOUR WELL

The most selfless thing you can do is fill up your own inner well. So many of us are running around half filled up. We subconsciously look to things around us to give us the nourishment and nurturing that we so crave. But the truth is no one can fill up your well but you.

You are no good to anyone if you're running on empty. Nothing can grow in barren lands. The feminine is bountiful, fertile, and rich. Tend to your own well and watch as the amount you have to give to those around you multiplies.

If your well isn't full you will find yourself craving things from the outside world to fill it. This is our body's instinctual way of reaching for the grounding and nurturing that we are not allowing ourselves to receive. Addiction is the absence of the feminine. And if your feminine is absent, your inner well is parched.

If you ever have the delight of visiting the Chalice Well Gardens in Glastonbury, you will find the best visual metaphor for tending to your own inner well. Visualize it now if you like.

As you sit in the gardens, you are soothed by the soundtrack of the red springs bubbling from the depths of the Earth. Drawing its waters from the womb of the Great Mother. The red springs are so bountiful it feels like they will never, ever run out. Flourishing, radiant, abundant, and eternal. There is more than enough to go around. Drinking these sacred waters, you can feel the water nourishing you as it works its way through your system.

The red springs are a metaphor for how we should all be living. We too have an inner well that's as bountiful. We mustn't just ration ourselves to what we need to survive. We must fill ourselves up until we overspill. And then offer some of that abundant plenty to those around us. The more overspilling your chalice, the more there is to go around.

What nourishes you? What refuels your body? What is nectar for your soul? What brings you back to life? What is your secret medicine? What makes you feel abundant and fertile?

It may be gardening, arranging flowers, getting a massage, using luxurious essential oils, snuggling up on the couch, hiking, sipping cacao, attending a woman's circle or yin yoga.

What nourishes me is cooking soup from scratch, watching the ocean roll in, going to the movies, stretching on my heated tiles, spa breaks, intuitive dancing, chats with like-minded sisters, creating for creating's sake, spontaneous bike rides, exploring somewhere new, visiting sacred sites...

What nourishes you is your medicine. When you give yourself the medicine that you need to nourish your soul, your soul nourishes all those around you.

RISE SISTER RISE

How full is your inner well now? Is it empty,
half full, full, or overspilling?

What needs to happen for it to be overspilling and full?

What nourishes you? Write a list of
five things that nourish you.

△

She realized that if we were going
to heal this global family,
She had better start with Her own.

△

HEALING THE MOTHER LINE

Until we are able to nurture and mother ourselves we won't be able to receive the nurturing and mothering that we have been longing for ourselves. The more we look to other people, or the world around us, to fill us up, the longer we will feel undernourished, parched, and like we are running on empty. Are you mothering yourself?

As our planet, our great Mother Earth is starving and crying out for help, so too are we. We all need mothering. And so many of us (your mother included probably) have been starving for it. The planet as a whole when in balance has the capacity to nourish and nurture our every need. As each of us honors our feminine by nourishing and nurturing ourselves, we are able to do the same for others. However, if we stay here in a victim/blame mentality about all the ways our mother didn't mother us or meet our standards of mothering we will never receive the nourishment that we so deeply crave.

If you didn't receive the nurturing you needed from your mother, chances are she didn't receive it from hers, and on and on it goes. Instead of listing all of the ways that she did not meet your needs, choose to meet your own. To treat yourself with the same compassion, love, devotion, and attention that you longed/long for. And while you do it, send some of it to your mother. Because if you need it, perhaps she does too.

The mother–daughter relationship has got to be the most complex of them all. Most women do all they can to resist the fate of 'ending up like their mothers.' But for most, the path is inevitable. We must stop blaming the woman who birthed us and instead celebrate that they did. No matter how brilliant or flawed, compassionate or cold, smothering or neglectful, it's important for us to acknowledge that they were doing the best they could with the tools they had, the times and conditions they were living in, and the mothering that they received themselves.

If we are to heal Mother Earth, we must start with healing the relationship with our own mothers. To acknowledge her sacrifices, to recognize her journey and to open our minds to the possibility that there was a reason that we chose her to birth us into this world.

RISE SISTER RISE

What sacrifices did your mother make for you?

What are you most grateful for about your mother?

What important lessons did she teach you?

What did you yearn for growing up that your
mother was not able to give you?

Why was she not able to give this to you?

How can you give this to yourself?

What do you yearn for from your mother now?

How can you give this to yourself now?

What does your mother yearn for?

If your mother was your child, what would you
want to give her, teach her or say to her?

What strengths does your mother have that you can call upon?

What pattern, way of being, beliefs, or method of survival did/
does your mother have that you choose not to carry forward?

What are you carrying that is not even yours?

What do you need to do to break this chain?

How can you mother yourself?

BREAKING THE CHAIN

Under the title 'The Strength of My Ancestors,' list all of the patterns, beliefs, traits, and ways of being from your lineage/family line that you choose to be strengthened by. Under the title 'Breaking the Chain,' list all the patterns, beliefs, traits and ways of being that you choose to release because they are no longer necessary or yours to carry.

**THE STRENGTH
OF MY ANCESTORS**   **BREAKING THE CHAIN**

△

THE IMPORTANCE OF RITUAL

*'We do not believe in the Goddess – we connect with
Her; through the moon, the stars, the ocean, the Earth,
through trees, animals, through other human beings,
through ourselves. She is here. She is within us all.'*

STARHAWK

You do not need to be religious, new aged or witchy to partake in a ritual or ceremony. All you need to be is open to being transformed by it.

A ritual can be as simple as writing down what you are ready to let go of and burning it in the presence of a full moon. It can be whispering your heart's deepest prayer into a crystal or putting on a music track and dancing to your prayers.

I do a simple ritual every day before I sit down to write.

I start by lighting (fire) some natural incense (earth) in my cauldron (a fire-proof bowl), while saying the following prayer from *A Course In Miracles* (a spiritual text focusing on love, inner peace and forgiveness) invoking whatever spirits, Goddesses, or guides I am working with to write through me on that day. Then I open the door to allow fresh air to fill the room (air) and fill my antique Mother Mary Holy Water chalice with a little bit of water I have from the Chalice Well (water).

Through ritual and ceremony we are in effect taking a moment to recognize and invoke the sacredness of Life. To take the time to mark a transition that has happened, is happening or that we would like to call in. I like using the four elements (earth, air, water, and fire), but you can use one or none.

When we gather in a meaningful open way, our heart and soul can feel it and are nourished in ways unknown to our mind. It is in the sacred space opened in ritual and ceremony that our remembering is deepened and we have the potential to connect with the soul of all things. We allow ourselves to be held by the force that weaves our lives. What happens can be felt but not seen. It cannot be measured except in the stretching of the heart. Each time we enter into a ritual or ceremony, we are connecting with all the people who have ever come together in that sacred way. In the West, ritual and ceremonies have been fading out of our lives but I believe they are making an important comeback.

Before getting married, I made the request to my closest friends that instead of having the classic hen party with splitting headaches and penis straws, I'd much prefer a handful of us come together in ritual (don't worry, we did the champagne thing too).

The first was in Glastonbury, England as I described earlier *(see page 31)*. The second was two days before my wedding in Sydney with my friends Jaqui, Amy, Sheila, and Robyn; my mum, and my Nanna Peg.

We had a ball of wool that we passed around the circle, symbolizing the weaving of love, support and wisdom as the seven of us gathered. Passing the ball of wool around the circle, each woman shared stories from their family lineage about marriage.

Jaqui spoke of how her grandfather never stopped adoring her grandmother; even in their old age they would still have G&Ts on the balcony every Friday at 5 p.m. and when looking at each other had that sparkle in their eyes.

Amy spoke of the courage of her nan who, after knowing her husband for only three months, decided to trust her heart, leave Scotland, and board a boat to Australia – a strange and exotic land on the other side of the world.

Sheila spoke of the importance of respect, being flexible, that you can break the cycle, and the importance of not always needing to be right.

Mum spoke of the strength I could draw from so many couples that while enduring so much still found the resolve to stay together through the ups and the downs.

Robyn spoke of the importance of lightness, how to see the funny side of things, and the thin line between extreme emotions such as anger and hysterical laughter – and that at those moments, always choose laughter.

Nanna sat there as the true matriarch, the Crone of the circle. We each listened with open hearts as she did her best to condense almost a century of living into a moment. Whispering stories of famine, war, strong women and men. As she spoke of my mother being born a light filled her face and my own mother visibly softened and started giggling like a little girl, revealing a part of her that I had never ever seen. Nanna had us all in tears. Flitting from story to story stopping occasionally to apologize for speaking for too long. Each of us encouraging her to go on, go on, please go on.

The separation between us faded as we held the wool that had woven our hearts together. In sharing stories and ourselves we all grow richer.

When Nanna finished, she looked at me directly and said, 'Becky, you come from a lineage of very resilient men and women. May you feel their strengths in your bones. And may you also feel their faults, of which there were many, because it was their good that allowed them to get through all that too. I hope that your life is much easier than theirs but may you always draw strength from their resolve.'

I felt her words with all of my heart and in that moment understood how I had learned to be such an endurance runner through life. I thanked my ancestors and decided that I didn't need to keep enduring like they had, but that I could draw on their strength as and when I needed it.

Two days later on my wedding day as I walked up the aisle with these six incredible women by my side, I not only felt them with me but I felt the strength of the men and women who had come before them. As I stepped over the threshold into marriage, it was all the richer as I was armed with their stories, wisdom, strength, and light that I could draw on in challenging times.

All of this from one short hour of my life in the form of ritual.

RISE SISTER RISE

How can you incorporate ritual into your current life?

Sign up to the *Rise Sister Rise Sisterhood* to receive rituals and mediations every month www.risesisterrise.com

Δ

The world was filled
with Her rememberings.
Waiting patiently to be

found.

△

JOURNEYING TO SACRED PLACES

So many of us are being called back home. To sacred lands that our souls once walked in different shapes and forms. Sent forth to pick up ancient memories and seeds of light planted there. The Earth holds secrets of times past. Do not be surprised if you are led. I see spontaneous pilgrimages in your future.

The veil of silence has been lifted. Her whispers are becoming easier to hear. We must listen with our hands, hear with our hearts and see with our ears, as the veil between the worlds becomes thinner by the hour.

I believe that rocks, trees and crystals store ancient wisdom from long-forgotten times. Times where we knew much more about surviving in harmony with this planet than we do now. Ancient wisdom from getting it right and ancient wisdom from getting it wrong. Crystals from lost periods of history such as Lemuria are rising up through the Earth's crust all over the planet. As if right on cue for these urgent awakening times.

RISE SISTER RISE:

What part of the world are you being called to journey to?

Δ

She traveled to

the   ends   of   the   Earth

to find the
COURAGE

to be who
SHE ALWAYS WAS.

Part IV
UNBINDING THE WISE, WILD WOMAN

'We are the Granddaughters of the
witches they couldn't burn.'

Unknown

△

THE SUPPRESSION OF THE FEMALE VOICE

Just a few hundred years ago I would have been burned at the stake or drowned for the work that I do now. And certainly for writing this book.

So many of us have a deep-seeded memory of these dark times. Memories of persecution for sharing your voice and truth. Ages where it was not safe for us to honor our feminine power, opinion, and capacity to heal.

I've seen it time and time again with my clients and students. Women and men with a knowing that there is something that they long to share – whether that be through writing, speaking, working in the healing arts or just stepping up in their current life – coupled with an unshakable and irrational fear to do so. If you relate to this fear of rising up into the work that you came here to do, I want you to know that there has never been a safer time in history for you to do this work. This is the time we have been incarnating for.

You stand on the shoulders of so many.
Feel their strength. Feel their gall.

It's time to call back your wisdom, to call back your voice. To embody your power and share your unique light with the world. Don't dim to fit in. Don't wait until you feel safe before you show the world who you truly are. Do it now. We are waiting for you. As you rise up it makes it easier for your sisters to find you. Those who are just like you. Those who are looking for you too. Across the planet many women are still persecuted for speaking out or expressing their beliefs or desires, but much has changed. It is time now to come out of hiding. If you can't find the courage to do it for you, do it for those who do not have a voice.

This is the time that we have been training for. It's time to draw strength from those lifetimes where your voice may have been silenced and life drawn short. It is safe to step out from the sidelines and let your luminance radiate in full. It's time to release and relinquish all ancient vows of silence taken by you or others. Come out from the sidelines. Be seen. Be heard.

#RISESISTERRISE MANTRA

It is safe for me to release and relinquish all ancient vows
of silence. It's safe for me to open the front and back of
my heart. It's safe for me to rise up and do the highest
and boldest version of the work that is calling me.

RISE SISTER RISE

How are you silencing yourself in your current life?

Is there a part of you that is keeping your brightness dimmed?

What is it that you are afraid of?

Are you ready to release any fears you have
around freely sharing your voice?

△

THE MYSTIC ALWAYS RISES

As she let her soul sing, She let go of lifetimes of silenced
truth missiles cemented in the deepest caverns of her soul.
A voice snubbed out for centuries, for saying too much,
for standing up too much, for being too much.

Her Shakti and wisdom restrained for centuries, but not anymore.
She could not be locked away, muted,
restrained or contained any longer.
Not now. Not ever again.

As she let her spirit move her, She danced right through the flames.
Resentment, anger, and rememberings stomped out with
every blazing convulsion, sway, and kick.

The movement created space for their tears, which flowed deeper than
all of the lakes they were submerged in through all of the ages.

Soothing and healing the burnings that once enveloped her bodies.
All of their bodies. All of our bodies.
Never forgetting, but still rising.
Just as She planned to, just as We planned to.

Sensing Her in the distance, one by one her sisters joined in,
knowing this dance by heart.

Standing taller from all those who came before and
those who chose to come again.
Who had lived the story of Her fall.
now returned to watch Her rise.

Rise Sister Rise.

$\triangle$

FINDING MARY

'I am the first and the last. I am the honoured one and the scorned one.
I am the whore and the holy one. I am the wife and the virgin.
I am the mother and the daughter.'
The Thunder, Perfect Mind

There was something in me that knew there were secrets hiding within names. Words that seemed to be a bunch of letters that could actually be treasures waiting to be discovered. Like an explorer in the 1900s I've been known to inquire into and unveil the meaning of names, for each of my clients and, of course, myself.

I discovered that one of the Hebrew meanings for Rebecca is 'bound' or 'to bind.' It was not until 18 months ago that I truly understood what that meant. The unraveling of this word has resulted in this book. I had always questioned how women were portrayed in the Bible. While most would roll their eyes when it was time to learn about Jesus from the nuns in religious education classes, I experienced feelings of interest and uneasiness. There was something deep in my heart that believed and another part that could not digest what I was being told. So I went on my own Christ journey. Reading lost scriptures, gnostic texts, and channeled material. Discovering Christ energy for myself, the presence of Mother God, the story of Avalon and the Priestesses of Isis, drawing my own theories around the connections with the ancient world of Lemuria (Mu) – the motherland.

I was relaying my journey to my friend Hollie Holden after she had just gotten back from a Holy Land Cruise. Fascinated by her pilgrimage I told her that I felt there was something hidden in the name Mary. Hollie then shared with me that one of the lesser-known meanings of 'Mary' is 'female Rabi' (meaning female scholar or teacher, Priestess).

I believe that Mother Mary was a virgin in the ancient sense (*as described on page 69*). A woman one-in-herself. Powerful. A teacher. An initiate of the Essene and Isis mystic schools. An embodiment of Shakti. A Priestess. A sacred vessel and keeper of the grail (the grail is within you).

I believe that Mary Magdalene was not just one woman, rather many High Priestesses ('Mary' meaning female teacher, 'Magdalene' meaning high tower).

There is so much hidden wisdom, messages, coincidences, and memories waiting for us to unlock at this time. Like the fact that 'Isis' is the name of the Egyptian Goddess and the fundamentalist militant group, highlighting the great polarity of our world in current time. The truth is unveiling before us as our consciousness lifts. Just yesterday I made a little discovery of my own. I've had this antique French Divine Mother holy water statue on the wall in my office. I fill it with water from the Chalice Well Springs, as a ritual to invoke the Divine Mother as I work. I've had it for years but yesterday, as I poured in the sacred water, I saw something that I had not been able to see before. A very small pyramid at the center of the cross. Another Mother Mary statue I have has a crescent moon on it – the symbol the Priestesses of Avalon are thought to have tattooed on their foreheads.

History is dismantling and making way for Hers. It's time that we disassemble the stories that we have been told about women throughout history, that we stop taking what we are taught as gospel and endeavor to discover our own truths.

RISE SISTER RISE

Are there any hidden secrets in the meaning of your name?

Δ

THE RETURN OF THE MAGDALENES

Before I began writing this book I was visited by a consciousness known as the Magdalenes. The Magdalenes are Priestesses from the Essene, Isis, and Avalonian lineages. Powerful mystics and female scholars trained in the healing, mystical, gnostic, Celtic, and sacred arts of Isis. They first came to me upon my first visit to the red springs in the Chalice Well Gardens in Glastonbury where the Michael and Mary ley lines meet. It was there that I was given the title and energetic download for this book. Upon my second visit I received more. My third initiation took place after a ritual with my friend Meggan Watterson.

For some time I kept it tucked away in my heart, not even telling my publisher because, to be honest, it felt so much bigger than me. How could I talk about embodying feminine power in full, when parts of me still denied her so? How could I write about unbinding ourselves when I was still unraveling? How could I possibly write about healing lifetimes of persecution when I was still to finish doing so myself? How could I write about being held by the Mother when at times I was still relying on my own strength?

But the Magdalenes kept coming back and I finally surrendered to the fact that the journey of rising is never done. As I described earlier, a surge of clients with a pattern of past-life persecution kept showing up for sessions. Real-life Magdalene sisters from times past began appearing in my own life, midwives destined to encourage and hold the space, as I unbound myself from my own patriarchal methods of survival, protection, and ways of being that this book demanded from me – from us, as we forge a new path for women into this new age.

The Magdalenes are not one woman, but rather an order of consciousness. Awakening in so many of us and rising all over the planet. Many of us ancient Magdalene initiates, Priestesses of Avalon, Isis, and Essene mystics who have been returning throughout significant periods of history to do the work of She.

Magdalenes are here to spark a new consciousness on the planet, one where the masculine and feminine are returned back to balance. Where the light of our soul is the thing that unites all. One where all people are reconnected with the sacred wisdom of their soul and within their womb and body. One where we surrender to the cyclic nature and natural rhythm of Life.

Magdalenes are here to remind others that it is safe now to share our voice and come out of hiding. That it is safe to open the front and back of our hearts. That it is safe to trust our inner wisdom and ancient knowing. That it is safe to embody our power in full force. To stop striving and soften. To choose pleasure not pressure. And to release the old identities that once served us without judgment.

Most Magdalenes have always been aware of their divine nature, embodying a certain remembering that there was something that they came here to share. Magdalenes are ancient souls who have a certain unshakable remembering of a time long before, where life on Earth was in complete harmony, many incarnated in ancient motherlands such as Lemuria, ancient Egypt, Atlantis, and Avalon. Living in community where all people were appreciated for their true nature. Where women could be trusted and not seen as competition. Where heaven was a place on Earth. In their deepest hearts, Magdalenes believe that this is possible once again. This is why so many have returned.

Magdalenes are here to gently yet fiercely rock each and every one of us back to harmony with the Mother (Earth). A Magdalene's heart is both gentle and fierce. She has the capacity to hold so much. A Magdalene sees beyond doctrine and recognizes the golden thread weaving through every religion. For this reason she may struggle with choosing a specific faith; however, she is a believer and her faith is unshakable.

Magdalenes are able to hold space for another without saying a word. Their energy is able to transmute and recalibrate things back to congruence. Strategically placed all over the world, many Magdalenes have a gypsy spirit, knowing when it is time to move. As if guided by a force beyond themselves, they just knows where they need to be when, even if the logical mind takes some convincing.

Magdalenes may hold great grief from times when their voice and the voice of others was silenced and snubbed out, and indeed in parts of the world still is. It is this that Magdalenes are here to heal.

With the world in the state that it is in it is easy to get overwhelmed and feel like there is nothing we can do or that what we are doing is never enough. However, we must remember that the way to heal this planet is first by healing ourselves.

The Magdalene consciousness is (re)awakening in us all. It doesn't matter if your path involves reaching many or just healing yourself. No work is more or less holy. It is time for us to activate the light that we so long ago planted. To activate, embody and anchor it in whatever pocket of the planet we are situated. To free all parts of the feminine that have been bound.

Unbound, unbound, forever unbound.

△

UNBOUND, UNBOUND, FOREVER UNBOUND

After working with the Magdalene consciousness that was rising within me for a while, I could feel a fiercer, more powerful, and potent feminine, bubbling beneath the surface. One who while She may have been bound or contained in the past was now readying herself to rise.

On one of my trips to Glastonbury I went to the crystal shop 'Stone Age' looking for something to anchor this new powerful feminine that I could feel rising within me. While I was there a large, dark moonstone ring called my name. It looked more like a sorcerer's ring than my normal light-filled Virgo Priestess style. A mirror for the darker unclaimed feminine, my Scorpio rising.

A couple of weeks later my friend Meggan Watterson arrived in London after her own returning to Glastonbury. Within a few seconds of meeting each other in the hotel lobby, she grabbed my hand and questioned: 'Where did you get that ring?' She later revealed that she had seen the same one in her dreams and even looked for it while she was in Glastonbury.

After a few sips of red wine in the hotel bar, we went upstairs to Meggan's room to get on with the sacred work we do best, by performing a ritual for each other. Using rose petals, rose oil, Chalice Well water, sage, and candles, we held space for the other. For my ritual we focused on releasing any way I had been keeping my power and soul's voice bound.

As Meggan placed the blessed water on my third eye, throat, and heart, and glided sage around the back of my heart she whispered, 'Unbound,

unbound, forever unbound.' I could feel the lifetimes of built-up protection continue to fall away making space for my ferociously rising unclaimed power.

That night a loud bang in my bedroom startled me awake. Sitting up I discovered that my diary (which I'd left on the nightstand) was halfway across the room, lying there wide open, with the pen on top of it. Moved by a force beyond me, I scooped up the book and pen and began writing.

> We are the Magdalenes. You have been initiated,
> now go initiate others so they too can remember.
> We are here. We are here. We are here. Hear our prayer.
> We are here. We are here. We are here. Hear our prayer.

Without knowing it, I'd found myself in the sunroom with my harmonium chanting a song in full. I had only just started playing the harmonium and could barely play a chant let alone create one. I let myself be sung, as though receiving some sort of recalibration and initiation while allowing them to sing through me. I looked at my phone and discovered that two hours had passed, but it felt like 10 minutes.

A week later while in Chicago I had the most amazing dream. I was shrouded in cloth and surrounded by my Magdalene sisters. Meggan was there, so was Madeline, and many others who had been part of my journey of unbinding, reclaiming, and rising. Some I knew by face, some by soul. Priestesses of Isis, gathered around me, lovingly, carefully unraveling the cloth that had me bound for so long. This cloth representing all of the ways I had kept my own power bound, presence contained and wisdom silenced. Layers of protection, necessary in the past but not anymore. As they unraveled the cloth, they placed soothing herbal oils over my body while whispering over and over again,

'Unbound, unbound, forever unbound.'

When I awoke the next morning, the sun warming my face, I knew something significant had shifted. While putting on my mascara I notice hundreds of beams of light dancing all around the room. The whole room, a mirror ball. Trying to work out where these beautiful reflections were coming from, I eventually discovered that the light was being reflected off the gold, sequined wings on the back of my Victoria's Secret angel winged hoodie.

I burst into tears feeling the presence of all the Magdalene sisters who had been part of this healing. Lifetimes in the making. Feeling their presence and knowing that when we feel safe enough to open the front and back of our heart our light is shared without effort or burden. I felt a weight lift off me. I knew it no longer needed to be hard and it was once again safe to open the back of my heart. That I was ever held and that I didn't need to do this work in hiding or on my own anymore.

A week later, at the Mind Body Spirit Festival in Birmingham, I was finally, at long last, no longer afraid to speak.

△

SPIRITUAL CLOSETS

With all of the persecution that has gone on over the past few thousand years, it's no wonder that so many of us find ourselves in a spiritual closet of some sort. It took me 17 years to step fully out of mine! I've come to discover that those who step into spiritual closets don't do so because they doubt their beliefs, rather they do it because their beliefs are such a big part of who they are. And the spiritual closet is a form of protection from being rejected for who they truly are.

I'll never forget the day I began to see the hilarity of hiding out in a spiritual closet. Prior to this, my spiritual books would be always hidden away in my handbag. One day at work I was searching for something in it and emptied the contents onto my desk. One of my male colleagues read the title of the book and made a harmless joke. I scooped up the book and hid it away again feeling like I had just been outed and judged.

About 10 minutes later he emerged from the bathroom dressed head to toe in cycle gear ready to ride home. I made a playful remark highlighting his nappy bike pants and clippy-cloppy shoes like I always did. He laughed it off and wished me a good night. In that moment I realized that there was no difference between my passion for the soul and his passion for cycling. He didn't take anything I said personally, so why should I?

We must not waste our time hiding parts of who we are from the world around us. It is our weirdness, our secret passions, our deepest beliefs that make us who we are. Come out of whatever closet you are in.

RISE SISTER RISE

Where in your life are you hiding?

What would happen if instead of hiding,
you allowed everyone to see you fully?

Δ

While they may have been successful in
~~silencing one,~~
Her voice
echoed on
echoed on
echoed on
echoed on
echoed on
echoed on
echoed on
echoed on
echoed on
echoed on
echoed on
echoed on
echoed on
echoed on
echoed on
echoed on
echoed on
echoed on
echoed on
echoed on

$\triangle$

RECLAIMING 'WITCH'
(THE NATURAL WITCH)

'I am a witch, by which I mean that I am somebody who
believes that the Earth is sacred, and that women and
women's bodies are one expression of that sacred thing.'
STARHAWK

'You're a witch.'

What if that were a good thing? What if being a witch was not something to be accused of, rather a title we claimed proudly?

An acknowledgment that you draw your strength from deep within, rather than an external source. That you know how to work with the powers of the Earth and Universe to manifest what you desire. What if it meant you were in touch with your feminine wisdom, that you owned your authentic power and were not afraid to show it? What if it meant you lived your life in deep reverence to and in flow with the cycles and rhythms of the moon, the tides, the seasons, nature, and Life?

Wise Woman. Wild Woman. Empowered Woman.

That you were interesting, opinionated even and unafraid of speaking your truth. That you believed there is magic inside you and every person too. That you believed in the power of ritual, the four elements and your ability to be transformed. It is time that we reclaim 'witch' and show that it is not something to be afraid of. Not in a hipster trendy way, rather in a way that honors the potency of who you are and the women who so courageously paved this path before us, regardless of the consequences.

Most people confuse the practice of Wicca with witchcraft. However, what I refer to as Natural Witchcraft dates back further than all of the great religions. Natural Witchcraft is the worship of Mother God and her seasons. As seeing all of life as sacred. Of tapping into the power and wisdom that we have within each and every one of us.

If all women were in touch with their inner wisdom and unafraid to own their natural power then the world would be a very different place. If all women surrendered to the Earth's natural rhythms, this planet would be so much more harmonious. Let's wipe clear the propaganda of the Middle Ages. Let's lift the stigma of the witch and allow its meaning to return to one of empowerment.

Let's reclaim 'witch' from being something we need to hide, to something that we can proudly own. Let's come out from the shadows and unleash the light that we have been doing our best to keep protected for fear of being misunderstood or harmed.

Let's make being called a 'witch' mean someone who knows her power, trusts her intuition, and isn't afraid to share her authentic magic and medicine with the world.

A wise woman. An awakened woman. An empowered woman. Someone who knows how to heal herself and others.

I am a Natural Witch. If you are reading this, chances are you are too.

Come out from hiding, you are needed here.

RISE SISTER RISE

Are you a Natural Witch?

How are you playing small for fear of
being misunderstood or judged?

△

HEALERS, WE NEED YOU

To heal is to make something whole again. A healer holds the vibration of wholeness and invites the other to see that too. To believe in that. To surrender to that. To choose that.

Now more than ever we need more healers to rise up. People who are able to see wholeness, not what is broken. People who can see the light in the darkness. People devoted to their own self-healing. People determined to see the wholeness of those they come into contact with. To encourage the butterfly's wings to grow rather than see them as stuck in a cocoon. To see the potential of what is possible, To nurse, stand beside, forge new paths and create art that inspires.

Healers don't just exist in the medical sense. There are other types too. Artists and mothers. Midwives and teachers. Singers and solicitors. Storytellers and bartenders. People who trust in their ability to heal the world around them by healing themselves. People devoted to nurturing themselves, others and this world back to wholeness. That is what makes a healer. The ability to see the wholeness of ourselves and all of Life. Heal the world. Surrender to your wholeness now.

#RISESISTERRISE MANTRA

I surrender to my ability to heal and be healed.
Instead of seeing what is broken, I choose to
see invitations to return to wholeness.

While She was

Just.

One.

Girl.

Her voice

was carried by

Many. Many. Many. Many. Many. Many. Many.
Many. Many. Many. Many. Many. Many. Many.
Many. Many. Many. Many. Many. Many. Many.
Many. Many. Many. Many. Many. Many. Many.
Many. Many. Many. Many. Many. Many. Many.
Many. Many. Many. Many. Many. Many. Many.
Many. Many. Many. Many. Many. Many. Many.
Many. Many. Many. Many. Many. Many. Many.
Many. Many. Many. Many. Many. Many. Many.
Many. Many. Many. Many. Many. Many. Many.
Many. Many. Many. Many. Many. Many. Many.
Many. Many. Many. Many. Many. Many. Many.
Many. Many. Many. Many. Many. Many. Many.
Many. Many. Many. Many. Many. Many. Many.
Many. Many. Many. Many. Many. Many. Many.
Many. Many. Many. Many. Many. Many. Many.
Many. Many. Many. Many. Many. Many. Many.
Many. Many. Many. Many. Many. Many. Many.
Many. Many. Many. Many. Many. Many. Many.
Many. Many. Many. Many. Many. Many. Many.
Many. Many. Many. Many. Many. Many. Many.
Many. Many. Many. Many. Many. Many. Many.
Many. Many. Many. Many. Many. Many. Many.
Many. Many. Many. Many. Many. Many. Many.
Many. Many. Many. Many. Many. Many. Many.

△

SET YOUR SOUL'S VOICE FREE

Now is the time to release your voice. To share your song. Expressing all of the things that your soul has to say. To be heard and to speak freely. Clear the chimney of your soul so those around you can hear the music you came to share. Let the sharing of your voice be your own medicine. Cathartic. And while you're at it, offer it up as medicine for those who lack the courage to do the same.

The days of persecution that your soul remembers are over. This does not mean that everyone will understand you or agree with you or even like what you have to bring. The more daring and true to your message, the more likely you will attract the attention of those who are not yet ready to hear you. But at least you will no longer be holding your magic inside.

When you share your voice, those who can hear you, who are waiting to hear what you have to say will flock to your side and sing along. Drinking up what you have to share like nectar. Cheering you on as you guide the way.

There are many who will be energetically activated simply by your decision to share. Your voice, igniting something indescribable in them. Set your soul's voice free.

RISE SISTER RISE

How are you being called to share your voice in a bigger way?

If you weren't afraid, what would you do?

△

RITUAL: RELEASING VOWS OF SILENCE AND CALLING BACK YOUR POWER

Light four candles and place them in a circle around you. One in front of you, one behind you, one to the left and one to the right.

Imagine a beautiful rose at your heart center, or hold a real one there. As you breathe deeply, imagine it opening softly and courageously, petal by petal. Call upon the power of Mother Earth to support you.

Imagine a stream of light connecting you to the heavens above, connecting you to the unified field of All That Is, while saying the following invocation:

*'Akashic Records Division, Magdalene Sisters, Priestesses
of Avalon and Isis, Durga, Kali Ma, all of the Marys,
Lakshmi, Saraswati, Shakti, and rising feminine energy,*

*I request the following in all dimensions,
past, present, and future.*

*Remove and render void any vows, contracts, bindings,
or ways I have knowingly or unknowingly chosen
to keep, or be forced to keep, my voice or power
restrained or contained in this life and any other.*

*Remove all layers of protection preventing me from stepping
into the full radiance of who I am and came here to be.*

*Sever all old identities and ways of being that may have served
me in the past but are no longer necessary in present time.*

Release anything that I am carrying that is not mine.

*It is now safe for me to step into my power in all
its potency and share my soul's voice authentically
and freely without fear or persecution.*

*I call upon the sacred masculine and Shiva
to protect me and my work.*

*In the highest good of all beings I trust this to be carried
out with joy now and in all aspects of existence.*

Thank you, thank you, thank you.

And so it is. And so it is. And so it is.'

After you have completed the invocation, don't blow out the candles, rather let them burn down and extinguish naturally. Keep them in place or put them on your altar or window ledge.

△

SOUL STORIES

We all have them. And many of us repeat them over and over again, lifetime after lifetime. The good girl, the martyr, the judge, the victim, the persecuted, the persecutor, the black sheep, the hermit, the mistreated, the cast aside, the one who is afraid to be seen, the one who is afraid to speak.

It doesn't serve us to keep living the same soul story over and over again. It is time to set ourselves free from the roles we have been playing even after we have learned the lesson. The thing about past lives is that they don't just exist in the past. If we don't release them, they exist in reality right now, and we end up living the same story over and over again.

So what's your soul story? What role are you playing in your life that you just can't seem to shake? What emotion or feeling or way of being is controlling your life?

May this be the lifetime that you say no to the pattern, to reliving the same thing over and over again. May this be the life that you shake it all off, liberate yourself from the stories of the past, and step into a new once upon a time.

RISE SISTER RISE

Ask the part of you that knows... Think about the greatest fear that holds you back in your current life. If you had to guess, what soul story or role have you been reliving over and over again?

△

PAST LIVES AND UNSHACKLING YOUR SOUL

You have incarnated more than once. Most likely lives over many eras. Perhaps you have even incarnated in ancient periods such as Egypt, Troy, Mesopotamia, or even ancient lands such as Avalon, Atlantis, Shambala, and Lemuria? There is so much that we don't know and so much we are still to uncover.

Significant past-life memories, particularly the traumatic ones, can be imprinted into our unconscious mind along with traumatic experiences from this life. It is from our unconscious mind that our beliefs, behaviors, and habits are formed. Therefore, traumas from past lives have the potential to influence who you are today if they are not processed and released.

Collectively many of us are healing past-life trauma due to living in the shadow of 5,000 years of patriarchy, while many other women hope for a future when they can do the same. Lifetimes where it was not safe for us to choose our own faith, where our bodies were not our own, where we were seen as second-class citizens and often the property of a husband, where it was not safe for us to speak out, share our truth, where open expression of our sexuality and passion was considered a sin.

It is time that we stop carrying around these ancient wounds and free ourselves to be who we truly are, not be bound by who we are afraid to be.

Our intention when working with past lives should always be to notice without attachment. If you were mistreated or experienced something traumatic, allow yourself to feel it and everything that comes with it, but resist the urge to carry on playing that role and living that story in this life. Take the wisdom, take the lessons, take the strength, but don't lose yourself in the drama of the story that you stop living this life you have now. Don't let your ego get in the way of unshackling your soul. Don't get stuck in the romance and drama of it. Resist the urge to let your ego get in the way saying, '*I was this famous person from history*'... '*I was a queen*'... or wallowing in the martyrdom of the suffering.

It is also important to remember that most of us have played the roles of both victim and villain. We have been the accused and so too the accuser. The persecuted and the persecutor. Keep your mind open and cast judgment aside. We all are made of light and shadow. Refrain from the urge to want to see only the light, for the shadow is often the thing that binds you tightest.

As we know better we do better. It is through making 'bad' decisions and becoming more conscious of our actions that we are able to become more aligned and certainly more free.

Recently I had a past-life experience where I actively journeyed into the shadow of my incarnation experiences. In other words, the lives you wouldn't want other people to know about. We all have them. I was inquiring over a pattern I had with a particular type of authority figure that no matter how experienced I got, I just could not shake. During this journey I experienced a past life where I turned on one of my teachers. It was only a matter of time until they found out and the waiting game was excruciating. As I watched the story play out I could feel myself crying. The tears released an ancient guilt and fear and I saw how holding on to it had resulted in me having this niggling feeling in my current life that I was always going to be caught out. I finally understood the feeling, this thing that was binding me and I was finally able to set myself free, releasing the previously unshakable pattern in my current life. What a relief it was.

Every past life I have journeyed to I have called back or released something that either frees or strengthens me. The artist and the healer. The adventurer and the initiate. The Chinese man who worked himself into the ground. The Isis Priestess and the Essene mystic who whispers in my ear 'unbound, unbound, forever unbound.' There are jewels and wisdom from times past waiting for you to uncover. As well as parts of you that yearn to be unchained so your freest self can be found.

My intention in looking at past lives is so that we can free ourselves from the way these past experiences are keeping us bound in our current lives. In looking at the shadow and the light we are able to release the chains that bind us, just as we are also able to call upon the skills and power that we have embodied before.

RISE SISTER RISE

Ask the part of you that knows:

If I had to guess, I'd say that a past life that binds me is...

What happened that your soul wants you to remember?

What advice does this part of you have for you today?

If I had to guess, I'd say one of my past
lives that strengthens me is...

What happened that your soul wants you to remember?

What advice does this part of you have for you today?

If you feel called to go deeper on your past lives, you may like
to try my 'Past Lives Journey' at www.risesisterrise.com.

△

YOU CAN BE SCARED AND STILL BE SAFE

It's OK to be scared. In fact, when it comes to rising, feeling scared or unsure is really quite normal. Especially when doing the work that your soul is calling you to do. Especially if you are called to forge a new way of doing things and transforming yourself. If you didn't feel a little bit unsure, that would be odd.

I've got a quote on my wall by Joan of Arc, which reads,

'I'm not afraid. I was born to do this.'

For so long I looked at Joan's fierceness and wondered how she could stand with such conviction. However, she is known for courage and courage isn't the absence of fear; it's facing what you are afraid of. When I feel into that quote now, I feel it is almost a mantra, assuring herself that she can do it, regardless of the fear. If you are afraid to transform, rise or pave a new path, that's my heart's deepest prayer for you. To find the courage to rise despite, and perhaps especially because of, the fear.

We are in a constant state of change. Each new moment is unknown. We do not know what is coming and we do not know what we are transforming into. The thing that makes it harder is resisting it. Like standing at the edge of the highest diving board and looking down. Stopping and taking in the sheer height and all the space between you and the water. The longer you wait, the more excruciating it gets. But if you move in one big sweeping motion, by the time you come up for air you say, 'That wasn't so bad, let's do it all again.'

This is the constant process of rising, of moving with Life. The longer you resist, the harder it gets. But if you allow the rhythm of the motion to take you, you start seeing it as a ride.

#RISESISTERRISE MANTRA

It's possible for me to feel scared and still be safe.
It's safe for me to open the back of my heart.

Every moment of every day we are to some degree standing at the edge of that diving board. The more you think about it and resist the inevitable, the scarier it gets. But if you allow the fear by breathing into it deeply and then leaping into the constant state of surrender, you begin swimming with Source. You become Source in motion. And when the water catches you, you discover that it is possible to feel scared and still be safe.

RISE SISTER RISE

What are you afraid to do that you have been avoiding?

△

LET SHAKTI SING YOU
(THE POWER OF CHANTING)

When you share your voice you unlock something in the Universe and call a missing piece of you home. Our individual voice is the most powerful sound current on the planet. If you have kept your soul's voice silenced or held back, chanting could be truly life changing for you. As we chant we don't just chant to free or heal ourselves, we also chant for all those who do not have a voice and the healing of all. In John (1:1) it says that 'sound or vibration is the most powerful force in the universe.' I couldn't agree more.

Chanting is the practice of singing divine names in repetition. It is a form of vibrational healing, as the sound current reverberates through your physical body bringing it back to harmony. The repetition of chanting causes our minds to get bored and rest, allowing another voice, our true voice, our soul's voice, to sing through us. If you have ever chanted or attended one of my workshops perhaps you know what I'm talking about. There comes a point in most chants where your voice actually changes. A resistance has been cleared away and created space for something sacred. Many times when I chant it feels like I both lose and find myself, my true self. For me, there is no other modality that has this same powerful effect.

There are 84 meridian points on the top of the mouth that are stimulated when we chant. These stimulate the hypothalamus, which stimulates the pineal gland, which stimulates the entire glandular system – which is why it makes you feel so damn good.

But more subtly, my favorite thing about chanting is the unified field that opens when we begin singing. It's as if the chant exists in that field on its own, and when we begin chanting we are instantly connected to it. And by being in that field through chanting along, you are also connecting yourself to all of the people who have ever chanted that chant throughout the past, present and future. That's a lot of divine support and holding.

Chants are more than just songs; they are invocations. We can direct them at specific ascended masters, Gods and Goddesses. All you need in order to call in their support is to put your intention into your singing. To invite their guidance, their presence. To open up and receive them walking beside you. Holding you. Loving you. Supporting you.

△

THE MOST POWERFUL SOUND CURRENT

'I'm a woman
Phenomenally.
Phenomenal woman,
That's me.'
MAYA ANGELOU

The following exercise is likely to make you uncomfortable. That's a good thing. In fact, the more uncomfortable it makes you, the more important it is to your rising.

These days we are bombarded with information from society telling us what we should look like, how we should feel about ourselves, where we should be, and even how to behave. Our bodies, our jobs, our wealth, our families, our career...

With so much noise coming at us, it's fairly impossible not to measure our value from these external forces.

However, as Maya Angelou so beautifully expresses in her poem *Phenomenal Woman*, there is a phenomenal woman ready to rise within each and every one of us. She doesn't need to change anything; She just needs to claim her magnificence in full radiance now.

There is nothing more powerful than your own voice. No authority has more sway. And the only way to be witnessed and celebrated by others is first to truly see, acknowledge, celebrate, and voice what is phenomenal about you right now.

PRACTICE: PHENOMENAL WOMAN

Write a three-page letter to yourself explaining why you are such an amazing woman. Why you admire yourself. What you are proud of. What have been your greatest achievements. Why you are a good person. What you have managed to overcome, to let go of, to rise above. Your greatest qualities and just generally why you are so amazing.

Record yourself reading your letter out loud on your phone or computer. This is the important bit. Do not wait for others to tell you you're good. Tell it to yourself and tell it to yourself now.

Listen to the recording every day for the next 21 days, and notice the significant change in your confidence.

RISE SISTER RISE

Do the 'phenomenal woman exercise' above. Do not overlook the power of this one.

△

TELL THE TRUTH ABOUT YOUR LIFE

*'What would happen if one woman told the truth
about her life? The world would split open.'*
MURIEL RUKEYSER

If you feel a certain way, rest assured that there are millions who feel the same. When I was young I thought I was alone in my desire to bring about this shift in consciousness and felt petrified to do it. I tried everything I could to overcome this fear before sharing my writing and voice. Then eventually I realized that my fear was part of my story and that if I felt this way, then others did too.

Slowing dipping my little toe in the water I began to share my writing. Eventually the words turned into chapters and chapters into books. When you tell the truth about your life, the good and the bad, you no longer have anything to hide. You free yourself. You show the world who you really are and 'your people' flock to you. The more honestly you share your voice and embrace your weirdness, the easier it is for your sisters to find you. If you keep your voice hidden, waiting for the fear to subside, your people won't be able to find you.

When you are honest about your life you give someone else permission to be honest about theirs. You give up the exhausting act of pretending you have it all together (which none of us actually do). When you share your story you set yourself and others free. When you are honest about your life you give yourself more space to enjoy it. Messy bits and all. And the messy bits are actually the most interesting bits anyway.

RISE SISTER RISE

How can you be more honest about your life?

△

YOUR LIFE IS YOUR MESSAGE

We are all connected. The only way to heal others is by first healing yourself. In my Work Your Light™ online course, I take my students through a process called 'Your Life Is Your Message,' where we look at key moments of their story and the things they needed to hear at those moments. It never ceases to amaze me how much this process works. Our life really is our message. And it is in letting the healing happen through us that we are able to have a healing impact on the world

Your message is the thing you most needed to hear.

When we devote our lives to rising, we are really committing to being the person we wish we had to guide us. When I write my books, I am not writing to convince someone else of a certain way but to the part of me that needed to hear what I now have to say. And, because we are all connected, there are others out there who will resonate with that too.

PRACTICE: YOUR LIFE IS YOUR MESSAGE

Get an A4 piece of paper and place it horizontally. Draw a line from left to right. This is your timeline. The far left is the day you were born and the far right is current time.

Plot out significant moments in your life. Moments that stand out. They can be little, perhaps a happy day with your family at the beach or huge, such as the death of your mother.

Go through each moment and ask yourself, what did you need to hear at that moment? And write it down.

Once you have completed all the moments, look back over your notes and see if you can find a common thread.

To all who were born
before their time:
That time is
NOW.

WHAT IS YOURS TO DO?

Often the path that is yours to walk is the exact
one that you do not feel prepared to walk.

Walk it anyway.

Often what is rising in us feels far bigger than
we feel we could possibly hold.

Be a container for it anyway.

Often our creations seem to have a wild
uncontrollable consciousness of their own.

Birth them anyway.

Often what is ours to do feels more like a challenge than a choice.

Choose it anyway.

Often what is ours to do is the very thing that intimidates us the most.

Be courageous and do it anyway.

She realized that the one
She had been waiting for,
had been Her all along.

△

YOU ARE BOUNDLESS

You are boundless. There is no end to what you are capable of. You are not your parents, you are not your civilization, you are not your sex or your sexual partners, you are not your story, you are not what others say you are, and you are not your mistakes.

You can try as hard as you can to limit yourself, but you will never wholly succeed. You are the divine daughter of a gentle expanding Universe that is cradling you every step of the way. The cosmos grounded for just a moment in time before the next metamorphosis. A breathing expression of light.

You can strive and scheme all you like, but no matter how much you force or resist, Life will never give up on finding ways for you to thrive. You are part of Life and Life always finds a way. Your time here is a fleeting moment. Don't spend your days resisting that which you are. Or comparing it to others. Surrender and let Life move you. Allow all that is inside you and bursting to come out.

RISE SISTER RISE

If you truly knew that you were boundless and anything was possible, what would you allow to happen?

△

UNTANGLE YOURSELF

'I don't consider myself a traditional person,
but a Universal person. Instead of abiding by
rigid rules, I want to be free in my heart.'
GRANDMOTHER FLORDEMAYO

As we go through life the things that we haven't been able to release tangle us up. Things we have taken on as a sense of duty. Things we have learned to be good at, but are not part of our true nature. The things that were once aligned to who we were, but are no longer aligned to who we are today. So we refrain from making a clean cut, binding ourselves to it for as long as possible, choosing not to choose instead.

As the years press on, the cords of the things we once clung to begin winding their way around our feet. Tripping us up time and time again, holding us down when we attempt to rise. Until one day we finally realize that until we untangle ourselves we will never be truly free. And that thing you are clinging to will never be free either if it continues to cling to you.

RISE SISTER RISE

What is tangling you up? What have you been afraid
to let go of? What is holding you back from rising?

There were no ropes
strong enough to keep Her spirit bound.

$\triangle$

THE UNCLAIMED SHADOW

True light and luminance are only possible once we have slept with our shadow. Just like the mighty oak cannot rise tall without first laying down an intricate root system deep into the Earth, we cannot truly rise if we haven't first looked at our underworld. Shadow work is not a one-time deal. We must tend to our garden on a regular basis, plucking out weeds before they take the nourishment that we need to grow.

Your shadow is your ticket home. If you ignore or banish Her, She will control you from within. If you listen to what She has to say, to what made Her this way, to what She was once denied She will tell you all that you need to set Her and you free.

The brightest of people I know are as bright as they are for they have embraced all shades of their human nature. The shadow is not something that we can use spirituality to rid ourselves from once and for all.

Our shadow possesses the exact thing that we most despise in others. For example, your shadow part may be afraid of sharing your voice. It may act out by not being able to be happy for people who are sharing theirs. You may even find yourself being annoyed and frustrated at people who are sharing theirs inauthentically. You can hide this part of you, or you can see it as an invitation. To admit that you are afraid. And to go about finding the courage to share it.

RISE SISTER RISE

What part of your shadow are you pretending does not exist?

How is this stopping you from stepping into your power?

△

WE HAVE A LOT TO BE
ANGRY ABOUT

'A wise woman wishes to be no one's enemy;
a wise woman refuses to be anyone's victim.'
MAYA ANGELOU

It's OK to be angry. Actually, it's more than OK. It's healthy. And holy.

We have a lot to be angry about. The state of the Earth. Being contained by a system that tried to extinguish the wild feminine spirit. The abuse of human rights that is happening across the world right now. Living in a society where women are taught to be ashamed of their bodies, if they don't fit into a certain shape, age, or size. Living in a society where the thing that happens to every woman every month of her life is made into something that should be taken care of but not seen. Unequal pay. The persecution of the witches and the propaganda that went with it. The persecution that still goes on today.

For too long women have been forced to contain their rage, keeping it all packaged up inside. But as the end of patriarchy draws ever closer, for many of us that box has flung open. And many empathic women are feeling the repercussions. Experiencing eras of repressed anger, resentment, rage, truth, and grief running through their systems. While it may feel uncomfortable, it is necessary for us to feel. For when we allow ourselves actually to feel the anger it makes way for something truly magical to happen – the anger has an opportunity to be transmuted into something useful: passion.

As with the most extreme of human emotions, there is a thin line between them. Anger and passion are made of the same stock. Both require us to give in to them wholly. Passion is not possible without anger being given the chance to roam free.

Passion is anger transmuted into positive action. Anger transmuted into passion makes creations happen. Instead of staying in anger (what you are against), find a way to transmute it into passion (what you are for). If you hold back your anger you will be holding back your passion. The world needs more passionate people. For passionate people are change-makers. I am not suggesting that we all go off on angry rants to anyone who will listen. Rather, I am saying embrace what angers you and express that anger in a way that is healthy, so that energy can be transmuted into something worth being passionate about. Passion has the potential to change things.

Let your passion be the drive to change things in your world.

Transmute the anger of what you are against into passion to create what you are for.

RISE SISTER RISE

What angers you most?

How can you transform that anger into passion?
(What you are against to what you are for?)

DIVINE MOTHER DURGA MA

Thank you for helping me feel all of the feelings
that I am not used to feeling
as uncomfortable as they may be.

Thank you for reminding me to offer them up to the
light rather than banishing them to the shadows.

And that sometimes it is necessary to cut things back
so that come spring they can bloom and rise.

And so it is. And so it is. And so it is.

△

CHANNELING YOUR INNER KALI

I first started getting in touch with my inner Kali back in 2010. As I approached my Saturn returns, my life started getting harder to hold together. I'd done exactly what a good girl is supposed to – study hard, go to uni, work hard, climb the ladder, find a relationship, blah, blah. And yet it all felt like nothing. As 2012 approached I could feel that at any moment it could all come crumbling down. The harder I tried to hold it all together, the more difficult it got.

I could feel a certain wildness start to encroach. This manifested in a lot of midweek drinking with my friend Amy Firth alongside me. It was pretty honest fun, but there was this reckless part of us that yearned for destruction. Like there was this ancient grief or rage that had not been given a voice and was causing us to act out.

One night when staggering through the streets of Fitzrovia, we gave this feeling a voice. I told Amy about an ancient Irish tradition called 'keening,' where it was customary for women to wail their emotions loudly. So we decided to give it a go in an effort to express all of the intense feelings we were feeling.

We started just by yelling a variety of reckless things and swear words out loud.

Amy then belted out, '*I'M A WWWHHHHHOOOOOOOOOORRRRRRRREE!!!!!!!!!*' as loud as humanly possible for as long as humanly possible. Once finished, we both looked at each other and fell to the ground laughing uncontrollably.

I then said, 'OK. My turn.' Taking a great deep breath I belted the same thing out.

'I'M A WWWHHHHHOOOOOOOOOORRRRRRREE!!!!!!!!!'

We both exploded into laughter again impressed and a little scared at the fierceness that the other contained.

This soon became our walking home ritual and indeed the best part of our night.

Years on, both Amy and I are healers by profession. We now joke that what we were really expressing while stumbling down those streets is:

'I'M A HHHHEEEEEEEAAAAAAAAALLLLLLEEEERRRRR!'

Sometimes the craziness is just feelings that for so long have been bursting to come out.

RISE SISTER RISE

Give it a go. Think about all of the pent-up emotion
that has been pushed down in you. Write it all down
and let it out with some good old Celtic wailing.
Better yet, invite a friend over and do it together.

△

CONTROL FREAK TENDENCIES

When we are trying to control things we are resisting the flow of life. Relying on our own strength. Trying to hold things in place for fear of what will happen if we loosen our grip. Believing that if we are not there to hold it together something bad will happen.

Beneath every control freak is a fear of letting go, a fear of not being supported, held, and looked after.

It is impossible to trust and control at the same time. It is impossible to play and be controlling at the same time. It is impossible to leap courageously and be a control freak at the same time.

You are supported beyond what you could possibly fathom. The only thing in the way of allowing yourself to feel this support is the belief that you are not. Can you find the courage and faith to leap? She is waiting to catch you.

RISE SISTER RISE

What in your life are you trying to control?

What is behind your controlling tendencies?

DARK MOTHER KALI MA

Thank you for rocking me and my foundations
when my soul cried for a way out.

Thank you for stubbornly burning down the tower
when I did not choose to leave on my own.

Thank you for continuing to rip away all of the layers of
protection so I had no choice but stand naked as I am.

Thank you for sending in wave after wave so that I know
with conviction I can ride whatever comes my way.

Thank you for serving up those who did not see
me so that I was forced to truly see myself.

Thank you for recruiting the haters so that I
could learn to cherish and love myself.

Thank you for sending those who would never understand
me so that I was forced to know and trust myself.

Thank you for delivering ones who overlook me so
I could discover how much I have to share.

Thank you for continuing to catch me off guard so I can see
all of the ways I attempt to protect myself from life.

Thank you for loving so ferociously no matter
how much I screamed and kicked.

Δ

She was so committed
To what was
Rising in Her.
That a part of Her
Died
And was
Reborn

Every.
Single.
Day.

△

ALL OF YOUR FEELINGS ARE HOLY

Give all of your feelings an outlet. Let them be here. They exist to be felt. Don't hold them in. Feelings held and buried are toxic. Every now and then we need to let our inner banshee reign.

Frustration expressed in the right way has the chance to be transformed into Kali-style power. Channel your inner Joan of Arc. Groan and stamp. Thrust your body and burn it all down. The rage or shame or whatever you feel is not sinful, it is actually quite holy, if you channel it right. Mourn for the loss. Express your disgust, at what happened or what should have happened or what could have happened; do whatever you need to do to let it all out. For us to be truly unbound and free, holding it in is no longer an option, release it we must.

I have a particular song that I put on whenever I feel frustration begin to build: 'Chandelier' by Sia. I scream and yell and sway and kick. And somewhere in that three minutes and 36 seconds, my frustration clears the way for something sacred to rise in its place.

The same can be done with a good old honest vent with someone who is able to hold the space for you without judgment. Take today for example. I was triggered by an email. My husband Craig came home sick from work and hopped on the couch next to me. Sensing my frustration, he asked me if I needed to vent about anything. Did I...

He held the space for what turned into a half-hour monologue. Before long the frustration turned into rage, which turned into shame. A little bit later the shame transformed into compassion. Soon after that the compassion turned into understanding. Understanding turned into insight, insight turned into inspiration, and inspiration turned into passion. Two hours later five new chapters of this book had been written.

Had I not allowed the Shakti to move freely, had I kept the shame in the shadows in an attempt to be a 'good girl,' had I kept silent, pushing the uncomfortable feelings down, I'd likely have sat at my desk all day feeling stuck, because the feelings and energy in my body would have been stuck. But now, I go to bed feeling free, supported, held, and grateful that I got to express myself so freely and it could be transformed into something productive.

Let all of your feelings have an outlet. Everything you feel is holy.

PRACTICE: TRANSMUTE YOUR FEELINGS

The only way to transmute your feelings is actually to FEEL them. If we do not allow ourselves to acknowledge and feel them they will keep us bound. But feelings are not the things that are trapping us, rather they are actually the energetic gate that can set us free. It is through feeling our feelings without losing ourselves to them that true healing and breakthroughs can occur.

1. Sitting in a chair or lying in bed, begin to breathe in really deeply while connecting with the earth that is holding you. Continuing to breathe really deeply, with your feeling eye start to scan your body from head to toe, allowing yourself to be drawn to a particular area.

2. Breathing in and out, notice what that area feels like. Without trying to understand it or do anything with it just allow whatever is there to be there wholly. Breathing in and out deeply, be curious and allow this feeling to be both emotionally and physically here. Notice how it feels.

3. How long has it been here? Is it yours or someone else's? How does it feel in your body? What color is it? What shape is it? How old is it? Is it new or ancient? Is it from

this life or another? What is it protecting? What does it want you to know? What triggered this feeling in you?

4. Breathing in and out deeply, allow your breath to transmute whatever is ready to be transmuted. Allowing it all to be here. Knowing there is nothing that you need to do, except allowing it all to be here because it is here. Your feelings and your body know how to heal themselves. Allow whatever is ready to fall away to fall away with your breath. Once the feeling has been transmuted continue scanning your body for other trapped emotions. Breathing deeply and allowing your emotional and physical bodies to do what they do best.

△

Steaming hot tears
streamed down Her face.
But instead of brushing them
aside She let them

F
A
L
L

F
R
E
E
L
Y

.

For a wise woman once
told Her that Her tears
were the most
healing waters of them all.

△

HOW DO YOUR SUBTLE BODIES MOST LIKE TO MOVE?

Naturally sporty, I was the kid who did pretty much every single sporting activity under the sun. From netball to dancing, tee ball to trampolining. I wanted to experience them all. Always outside climbing trees and learning the latest dance from music clips and Broadway musicals. However, ever since awakening, the physical body became the part of me that I put last.

Even when I was still a teenager, I would go to kinesiologists and healers who would want to work on the body but I was way more interested in the spiritual insights we could uncover. I remember seeing my body as a thing that was in the way, stopping me from experiencing everything that I was in such a rush to explore. As my journey and career progressed, I would much rather spend time learning and developing my emotional, mental, and spiritual bodies than my physical one. Looking back, I see how I was trying to be superhuman in a way. Bypassing the normality that comes with being on Earth and instead choosing to hang out in my emotional, mental, and spiritual bodies.

Even my addiction to coffee was an attempt to resist my humanness. Pushing my physical body to extreme productivity levels beyond what my body would naturally allow but my mental body demanded. It felt like I was always in a rush, like there was so much I needed to do while I was here that I needed to just get on with it. Knowing that my body was not reacting well at all to the coffee was not enough for me to ditch it. However, when I discovered that it was affecting my intuitive sensitivities and ability to manifest (because my energy was always so forward, and not in a state of receiving) I was able to wean myself off it in no time.

I believe that many old souls have a hard time being in a human suit. We get frustrated, and feel trapped and uncomfortable. We at times try to bypass the laws of Earth but in doing so we not only miss out on experiencing some of the pleasures that this planet has to offer, we are also not able to fully ground our energy, which is so necessary if we are going to have an impact here, no matter what we want to create. Physical movement is crucial for this. But instead of forcing yourself to go to the gym, consult your mental, emotional, and spiritual subtle bodies as well.

Our subtle bodies include but are not limited to our physical, emotional, mental and spiritual bodies. If we don't allow our thoughts, emotions, and traumas both current and past to be expressed in some way they build up and stay stuck. Stagnant. Blocked. For example, past-life memories are stored in the emotional body. In order for us to feel free and balanced, it's good to check into each of our subtle bodies and ask them how they most yearn to move in order to transmute any stuck energy.

After years of failed gym memberships, personal trainers, dumbbells, and Swiss balls, I have discovered that my subtle bodies most yearn for meaningful, flowing physical movement where I can move and express myself freely. I find that my creations actually depend on it. As I allow my body to release and fluidly move it's as if I am both strengthening my ability to be moved by my soul and unlocking wisdom within my physical body. The more I check into my mental, emotional, and spiritual bodies and allow them to move me, the more free I feel in my physical body, as if I am clearing the energetic fields around me and allowing them all to communicate together. Yin yoga, siddha yoga, kundalini yoga, walking in nature, and intuitive dance. It's taken me a while but I've figured out that these forms of exercise clear, soothe, and free my subtle bodies, and allow me to truly embody my soul and let Shakti move through me.

If you put me on a treadmill or in a spin class or a boot camp where the instructor yells at you I will shut down. Knowing what forms of movement your physical and subtle bodies most yearn for is powerful.

After being inspired by a friend I have recently picked up swimming as a devotional practice. Instead of doing the laps to lose weight or some other kind of outcome, I devote every stroke to being in harmony with the planet by chanting. My favorite chant for swimming is the ancient yogic mantra 'Ra Ma Daa Saa, Saa Say So Hung.' Here's the translation.

- Ra – Sun

- Ma – Moon

- Daa – Earth

- Saa – Impersonal Infinity

- Saa Say – Totality of Infinity

- So – Personal sense of merger and identity

- Hung – The infinite

It's a fabulous Kundalini chant for healing. While you are chanting it, you can send the healing to someone else, the planet, or yourself. With whatever chant I am doing at the time I imagine every single stroke gliding me closer and closer home to my true Self.

RISE SISTER RISE

Ask the part of you that knows:

What type of movement nourishes your physical body?

What type of movement nourishes your mental body?

What type of movement nourishes your emotional body?

What type of movement nourishes your spiritual body?

What type of movement are your subtle bodies most craving?

LETTING SHAKTI DANCE YOU

Your body has wisdom, memories, lifetimes locked in it. Those of your own and those of all of the women that have come before, in your direct lineage and beyond.

The more you sway, swing, circle, move, and shake, the more you unlock, unfurl, unwind, and unbind. The more you let your body move the way it longs to move, the more free you will feel. Let movement be your soul's medicine. Let the Shakti that is coiled within you rise and spiral free.

You are here to remember, uncover, and transmit it all. Don't dance from your head, dance from the depths of your ancient soul. Allow yourself to be danced. Let Shakti dance you.

Dance has been something that I always come back to. Like most young girls I did it growing up. But it wasn't until my mid to late teens that it began to be a soul practice. When I had the house to myself, I would put on the speakers and do what I called interpretive dance. I allowed my body to be moved by the creative force within me – bending, leaping, shaking, and moving in ways that just felt good. Studying for my exams I would give myself 'interpretive dance breaks' amazed at how recharged, free, and focused I would feel despite having been confined to my desk for hours on end.

At school dances I recruited some friends to be part of 'Becky's Dance Group,' which turned into a show of its own. We would dress up in theme (when there wasn't one) and claim our podium, where we would stay dancing all night. Much more exhilarated by letting Shakti move through us than chatting to boys.

During my 20s my dance practice lay dormant. And with every year, I found myself feeling more and more trapped. In 2010 I was reminded of my love affair with dance by one of my teachers and, as I reincorporated this age-old practice back into my life, I could feel the shackles start falling away. As I allowed myself to be moved by a force so much greater than me, I felt the Shakti begin to rise once again. I was not doing the dancing, rather She was moving me.

RISE SISTER RISE

How long has it been since you danced?

△

She danced because
She was grateful to be alive.
She was grateful to be alive
because She danced.

△

CHOOSING TO BE HERE NOW

'The long sleep of Mother Goddess is ended.
May She awaken in each of our hearts.'
STARHAWK

Earth is thought to be the densest place in our solar system. I often say to clients and students that if we can manage to turn our light on here, we can turn it on anywhere.

At soul level, we are used to being one. The earth experience however puts us in separate bodies. We experience polarity and duality and all that comes with being human.

Many feel the weight of being bound by our separate human bodies. The burden of being in a female body, having the rug pulled out from underneath us each month, especially through the past thousands of years of patriarchy where woman has gone unrecognized for being the divine vessel that She is. It's as if we have been doing this journey for such a long time, and are not sure how much longer we want to continue returning here.

If this is you, I want you to know:

This is the time that we have been incarnating for. While this planet may not be your original home, while you may find being in a human body difficult, while the state of the planet may not be aligned with your ideal experience of it, you chose to be here now. To be human now. To be a woman now. To bring back the feminine healing codes and free the feminine voice now. Now is the time for us to heal

our wounds and step into our womanhood. To initiate ourselves in the way we wish we were initiated.

In order for us to do this we must accept our humanness and all that comes with it and learn to be present in our bodies now.

Your feminine body holds so much wisdom. Wisdom that is waiting to be unlocked, as you give yourself space to breathe and receive it; wisdom that is waiting to be set free, as you give yourself the freedom to move and be moved. As you do this, the collective female suffering will be transmuted, clearing the way for all to hear Her call.

RISE SISTER RISE

How can you honor your human body more?

How do you wish you were initiated into womanhood?

How can you give this to yourself now?

Held by the Earth.
Moved by the Moon.
Sparked by the Sun.
Swayed by the Sea.
She was a force
to be reckoned with.

I GOT BODY

For women, one of the most significant ways we stop ourselves from stepping into our power and rising is through feeling something is wrong with us or that we are not ready enough because of the way our body looks. We live in a society that idealizes images of highly airbrushed distorted-reality women and looks at real women such as Lena Dunham and Amy Schumer as being 'plus sized,' when rather they are NORMAL – if not more slender than the average woman. With this constant bombardment of crazy body distortions fed to us through magazines and advertising, it's no wonder that most of us are running on a body acceptance treadmill that never ever stops. We say if I could just lose a dress size or three, then I'd be happy with my body.

We use food as a way to control life or as a way of numbing out our 'too muchness' (*see page 85*). I was recently on a girls' trip with fellow authors and journalists. Upon returning home I noticed a sadness in my heart. Inquiring into it, I discovered that it was because so many conversations kept coming back to weight, food, and appearance, revealing an inadequacy amongst so many of us about our appearance and body, including me. Now, the women on the trip were some of the most conscious women I know, which is why it was so saddening, that after all of the work we had each done, this inadequacy still existed.

Body acceptance doesn't mean getting to your ideal weight. It means loving and accepting your body as it is right now. You don't need to love your body but you can begin to accept it by choosing to see it with compassion and not comparing yourself to a distorted ideal that is not even real. Or just as bad, strive to reach the ideal size or shape that your were five years ago.

A little while ago I bought a Nintendo Wii, as I thought the dancing games would offer fun quick writing breaks. Upon setting up the Wii Fit board, the annoying thing took my measurements and pronounced out loud to the entire room (Craig and I), 'You are slightly overweight.'

F you! I thought. And went on a rant about how wrong it was that a stupid machine with a high-pitched voice was telling me what I should or shouldn't look like.

But when I sat with it I realized that the reason I was upset was because I hadn't accepted my own body. If I had, I certainly wouldn't have cared what a machine said. And when I looked at it, at a time in my life where so much had been going right and so much of my life had been demanding my attention, it was exercise that I had let slip. I knew this. I consciously chose this. But I was still expecting my body to remain the same as when I was exercising for an hour each day, or how I looked when I was 25.

The extra weight I had been carrying was made from very real things. Two years of celebrating being in love. Birthing two books into the world. And facing my lifelong fear of sharing my soul's voice with the world through my creations. Would I change any part of that? No.

We are living in a cyclic world. You are not meant to look a certain way for longer than that specific moment. We are ever-changing, cyclic beings who are here to experience change. To experience our soul in a human body over time. And human bodies are in a constant state of change. If we strive to reverse the clock or get back to a previous state we are going against the flow of Life.

In order to do the work we came here to do and truly rise, we need to be able to embody it fully, to hold the vibration of our message/calling/creations. And that starts with accepting our miracle of a body as it is, right now.

PRACTICE: I GOT BODY

Stand in front of the mirror naked for three minutes every day for 21 days. Pick a song or mantra ,such as '*Om Nama Shivaya*' (meaning 'I honor my true self'), to play each time if you like.

Now notice your inner dialogue, as you witness all of yourself in the mirror. Allow all of your feelings and judgments to emerge. This is the inner dialogue that you are carrying around with you. You are listening to it every day anyway.

Watch as your inner dialogue begins to soften to love and compassion the more time you spend in front of the mirror. Watch as your distorted image of the way you really look begins to shift back to reality.

You may also discover different parts of your body in which you are holding hurt, pain, anger, shame, or sadness. Where in your body you are holding in your feelings, holding in your voice, holding in your truth, holding in your bigness. Where in your body are you holding things that are not even yours? Your belly could be reminding you of a creation that is ready to be birthed. Your left shoulder could be trying to get you to rest more often. Your hips may be longing to dance.

Warning. This exercise has the power to change your life. Uncomfortableness will turn into acceptance.

△

YOU DO NOT GET TO DETERMINE MY WORTH

'Fate whispers to the warrior, "You cannot withstand the storm," and the warrior whispers back, "I am the storm."'

Unknown

Trees don't shrink and stand tall, according to who is standing beneath them. They own their greatness regardless. Flowers don't open and close according to who is walking by. They show their beauty regardless.

Don't let someone else's presence change your true nature. Do not let their power or skill change what is great about you. Do not let someone else's opinion of you change yours. Do not expand or shrink according to who is around. Do not allow situations or people to determine how tall you stand or how strong you feel. Do not change the size of your presence according to the bigness or smallness of someone else's.

Walk as though you are a mighty oak, open like you are a royal rose. Know that you deserve to be here just as much as anyone else. Do not draw your value on the number of followers or the title on your office door. Respect and admire your elders but do not give away your power to someone else. You need it for yourself. It doesn't belong to anyone but you.

If we are looking to another for any kind of approval we are giving our power away, saying, 'If you approve then I am.' But you already ARE all that you are, you do not need some external force to deem it so.

As I described earlier, patriarchal society has been built on a linear model of few leading many (*see page 76*). This model assumes that the few are better than the many. There is a big difference between respecting your elders, teachers, bosses, etc., and bowing to them in the hope that they recognize your worth. You don't need any external force to validate who you are. And you certainly don't need them to tell you who you are.

Four years ago someone I admired and had been looking to for approval failed to truly see me and questioned my worth. At first it upset me deeply. But after the ugly tears came and went, I discovered that they had just given me a gift. See, prior to this I had been looking to their approval. And in them failing to give it to me, it forced me to see and claim it for myself.

You know that moment... when someone says, 'You can't do that...' and a fire in your belly roars, 'Don't you tell me what I can or can't do...' Now, that's what I'm talking about.

RISE SISTER RISE

Who do you give your power away to?

In whose presence do you diminish your bigness?

Who do you not quite feel worthy of being around?

I SAY who breaks me.
And it's not gonna be you.

△

RITUAL: CALLING BACK YOUR POWER

Get a piece of paper and write down the names of any person, people, organization, or experience that you have either willingly or unwillingly, consciously or unconsciously, given or lost your power to in the past. Or anyone that intimidates you today. Write their names on the piece of paper.

In a fireproof bowl (or cauldron, if you have one) burn the piece of paper while saying the following out loud with conviction:

'I call back my power in entirety from anyone or any circumstance that I have given it away to in the past either willingly or unwillingly, consciously or unconsciously. The only one who says what I can or can't do is me. I call back my power in entirety now.'

Put on your favorite power song (mine is 'You Don't Own Me' by Grace, G-Easy) and call back your power as you dance, invoke, and embody your fierceness in full.

Part V

REDEFINING SISTERHOOD

'Another world is not only possible,
She is on Her way. On a quiet day,
I can hear Her breathing.'

Arundhati Roy

△

THE REUNION

Deep in the English countryside in a forest of silver birch, hazel, cherry, and oak, She found herself in circle with three women who truly saw Her.

Priestesses from times past. For so long journeying solo. At last, at last, reunited at last. Their parched souls yearning for the nourishment that only a sacred circle of sisters could provide. As they rested their weary foreheads, their second hearts opened in the deepest caverns of their wombs. Like sweet nectar they drank it all in. Everything barren and brittle brought back to life.

They took turns in revealing their most tender of wounds. The result of wandering on their own for millennia. Of doing this work alone. In hiding. Underground. Cut off from the sweet and nourishing ambrosia of their sisters' and Mother's song. Fumbling around in isolation, led only by the mysterious red lit thread in their heart. They wondered, How on Earth had they had survived all this time doing this work on their own?

They let their tears roll free, releasing lifetimes of persecution and layers of protection that were no longer necessary to hold on to. Not now. Not ever again. With each hot salty drop, you could hear their chalice replenish and overspill guilt-free. Wounds were soothed. So-called weaknesses alchemized into their own unique offering of medicine both for themselves and the world at large.

Together they initiated themselves into womanhood. Into Priestesshood. Just like they had in long ago lands that their soul remembered. Entwined by heart, they began to see the magnificent tapestry of light that they, we, She had for so long been weaving. Sisters. Priestesses. Recognized at last.

$\triangle$

THE ONES WHO CAME BEFORE US

'Suddenly all my ancestors are behind me.
Be still, they say. Watch and listen.
You are the result of the love of thousands.'
LINDA HOGAN

When you choose to rise, you never walk alone. When you choose to rise you tap into the collective strength of an ocean of women who, despite the circumstances, found the courage to rise. When you choose to rise you tap into a portal of sisterhood that, while invisible, can be deeply felt. You tap into the power of the Mother and the spinning of the moon.

They kiss the ground before you. They cheer you on from the rafters. Silently showing you the way. When you allow yourself to be held by their grace, you realize that even when you feel you might be, you never ever walk alone.

So stand with conviction. Walk tall on their shoulders. Let their voices carry. Dance unrestrained.

#RISESISTERRISE MANTRA

I allow myself to be held by the strength of those
who came before me. I never ever walk alone.

Goosebumps ran down Her side.
She knew that She was not alone.

She was held by all of the
sisters who came before Her.

Guided by their voices.
Strengthened by their gaul.

Δ

WHEN WOMEN CIRCLE

For ages, women have been gathering in circles to heal their wounds, share their stories, pass down the mysteries of womanhood, support and empower one another.

From ancient caves to coffee shops, moonlit dancing to WhatsApp group texts, stone circles to workshops. For longer than any of us can fathom, women have been tapping into the mystical power that is activated when women circle. It doesn't matter what our age, life experience, shape or size, when three or more women come together with a common sacred intention, you can be sure that something magic is about to happen.

Sharing stories, holding space, and a passing down of wisdom, there is nothing more healing than being in a group of honest sisters that truly see and accept you. In a period of history where we live more separately than ever, the ritual of coming together is one that we must not underestimate. In my experience it is something that all women crave but most aren't aware of. And when we get a taste of it we wonder how we ever survived without it.

The Red Tent by Anita Diamant gave voice to one of the voiceless characters in the Old Testament. The red tent was a place that the women of the tribe took refuge in at the full moon and where they found sisterhood, support, and encouragement from their mothers, sisters, and aunts.

I believe deep down we have all been yearning for that red tent. A place where we can be supported and held. Where we can share and be truly heard. Where we can let out our crazy without being judged. Where we can lay down our burdens and stop pretending to hold it all together. Where we can stop trying to do it all ourselves. Where we can be honest about how difficult life can get and how difficult it can be to be in a female body. Where we can have a conversation without someone trying to fix us. Where we can simply be and admit our deepest darkest secrets, and know that no matter what we confess we will still be seen and loved.

To keep the spirit and wisdom alive of those who walked this path before us through sharing their stories. To remember those that we have loved and lost and gather the courage to love again. To be strengthened by what others have been able to withstand and knowing that if they could maybe we can too. A place to swim in the sacredness of being a woman. And know that no matter what, we are never ever alone.

I believe that our society is starving for this deep feminine connection. I haven't come across a woman who doesn't yearn for it. This threading of support. This genuine female connection.

Without receiving genuine sisterhood, we remain girls. Competing with our sisters and endeavoring to reach an idealized version of perfection that is impossible to reach.

RISE SISTER RISE

Do you currently have a circle of women
that you connect with?

If you were to organize a circle of women to
come together, who would you invite?

Δ

YOUR CONSTELLATION OF SISTERS

'Because there is one thing stronger than magic: sisterhood.'
Robin Benway

When you make the decision to rise know this:

Your support team is assembling.

By answering the call that is in your soul, you are instantly connected to a group of sisters who have that shared mission. You may not be able to see them but there they will be. Like lights turning on all over the planet, your constellation of sisters spiraling around you. Comprised of those who have come before and those who are a couple steps ahead. United like an army.

As you read these pages, you are connecting yourself to an ocean of women rising alongside you. An invisible thread, a string of lights, a fierce unstoppable force. If you sink into the light in the depths of your heart, perhaps you can feel the flickering of their presence? From women who you have never met and perhaps never will.

#RISESISTERRISE MANTRA

I allow myself to be held and deeply supported by my
constellation of sisters. Both those I know and those
I have never met. When I rise they rise alongside
me. When they rise, I rise alongside them.

△

CALLING IN YOUR SISTERS

Until my late 20s I remember being surrounded by many friends and loved ones yet feeling so alone. And I couldn't quite put my finger on why.

I had an ancient memory of a sisterhood: A union where it was safe to share the deepest darkest parts of your shadow, as well as the brightest parts of your light. A healing circle of women whose purpose was clear. There was no separation of you or me, rather a sacred union of 'us' sharing our journey and doing the work together. I was searching for sisters from times past. Ones who already knew me. Ones who were looking and longing for me, just as I was looking and longing for them. Those who at soul level were made of the same stuff. As if a seed of light had been planted in each of us, like a homing device calling each other closer by the day. To do the work that we came here to do in unison.

I prayed nightly to find them. First came Angela. Next was Sheila. In both of these women it felt like I could see my own soul mirrored back to me.

However, at the time I couldn't help but wonder where were my sisters of my generation. I now see how while I was longing for them I was also in hiding, not showing those around me my whole self. Once I found the courage to step out and let myself be seen, they would find me and I them. Today I am blown away by how many amazing women of all ages I have in my life. More and more appearing every day.

The sisters you are longing and looking for are also longing and looking for you. Embrace your weirdness, own your potency and speak up so they can hear you.

RISE SISTER RISE

Who in your life is one of your people?

How can you let yourself be more fully seen?

△

GENUINE SISTERHOOD

'Your legacy is every life you have ever touched.'
Maya Angelou

Genuine sisterhood is the capacity to truly be there for another without expecting anything in return. To rest into the raw, sacred, vulnerable power of being a woman and witness the same in another without feeling inadequate. True sisterhood is our capacity to greatly honor another. To hold and be held. To mother and be mothered.

True sisterhood is bowing our entire being to the lineage of women who came before us and made up the very thread of all of Life. It's about owning the crazy, wild, and unpredictable parts of us and others without judgment. It's about knowing that our innate power is never drawn by cutting another down. It's about refraining from fixing and healing another, rather holding the space and their hand until they can find the courage to do it themselves.

Genuine sisterhood is more than merely supporting others through our words or mutual interest, rather it is measured by our ability to stay there at the raw, messy depths. Through the hurricanes, the floods and the fires. Genuine sisterhood is a powerful force. Untamable. Impenetrable. Unstoppable.

It comes from the soul. Age, family, country, color, background, life experience, or success don't matter. The heart recognizes a sister in an instant and the soul never forgets. A wild, raw, sacred, holy connection that cannot be forced or faked.

RISE SISTER RISE

Who in your life do you consider a true sister?

Who in your life do you spend time with
because you think you should?

Who is in your life because they want something from you?

Who is in your life because you want something from them?

△

CAN YOU HOLD SPACE FOR ANOTHER?

Can you hold space for another? Like really truly hold space for them? One of the most generous gifts you can give someone is your ability to be WITH them without trying to get them somewhere or get something for yourself.

To hold them energetically without turning the conversation back to you.

To refrain from saying 'me too,' 'in my experience,' 'I can so relate,' or 'how about this.'

To resist fixing, guiding, saving, or moving at a different speed.

To meet them where they're at and for that place to be absolutely OK.

To be the vessel for the Mother to enter.

To allow your arms and eyes to be the arms and eyes of the Great Mother, gently rocking them back home no matter how far they journeyed off course.

When you hold space for another, you allow them to move gently from their head to the heart. And if the heart feels safe and seen, you will witness the transformation of the soul stepping forth, which is an honor indeed. We all yearn to be witnessed like this. We all long for someone with the capacity to truly hold us.

RISE SISTER RISE

Can you hold space for others, without fixing them or turning the attention back to you?

Who in your life has the capacity to hold space for you?

△

THE NEW FORM OF PERSECUTION

*'The problem I have with haters is that they see
my glory, but they don't know my story...'*
MAYA ANGELOU

Feminism is so loaded. We must stop nitpicking our fellow sisters, especially in the name of feminism. If a woman says she is a feminist then every one of her actions is judged. If a woman says she is not a feminist then she herself is judged.

My friend has received complaints that she is putting feminism back by helping women reconnect with their monthly cycle and listen to their body when it tells them to slow down (so important!). While my other friend gets horrible comments saying that her extreme success is due to pushing down her feminine nature and choosing not to have kids.

As women we have had to fight for so much, let's not add another mountain to climb by having to rise from each other too. Before you attempt to cut another down, no matter how much you disagree, first take a moment and see if you can see a woman, who in **her own unique way**, is doing **her** best to find the courage to rise. Let's stop pushing our fellow sisters down no matter how much you agree or disagree with the way they are doing it.

Let's not turn on each other.
Let the persecution stop here.

RISE SISTER RISE

Who have you been judging harshly?

What's beneath your judgment?

Are you able to see her as a woman who is doing **her** best, in her own **unique way** to find the courage to step forward and rise?

Rather than focus on her or what she stands for, if you turn around the focus, is there something that you are being called to create?

△

IS SHE MAD AT ME?

How often have you sent a text or email and not received a reply, and then thought, *'She must be mad at me.'* This paranoid feeling is rooted in an ancient distrust between women. During the witch-hunts of the Middle Ages, people (particularly women) were forced to turn on each other in order to save themselves and their loved ones.

As women we have been also forced to push down the more powerful, darker parts of our true natures (as depicted in the darker phases of the moon and the related archetypes of the Wise, Wild Woman and the Crone, *see pages 117–118*) in order to fit into the box of a 'good girl.' So we have this 'other' part of ourselves – this shadow – that for many has been banished and unclaimed. And we think, if we have this part to us, then other women must too. Enter mistrust.

In a race to get the job, the guy, the best friend, we have learned to mistrust other women, assuming the worst.

So many of us hold old wounds and programming that causes us not to trust other women. To put up our defenses rather than soften and open. To gossip as a way of developing a deeper connection, in an effort to feel safe. We must stop the persecution of other women. The competitiveness and, most of all, the mistrust.

Being disconnected from the never-ending chalice within our womb, so many of us believe that there is not enough to go around. There is a part of us that remembers and yearns for deep and true connection with women. However, if we haven't healed our defenses and the unclaimed patriarchy that exists within us, then genuine sisterhood just isn't possible. We must heal our wounds around trusting other women.

We must allow ourselves to be supported and held, by other women and also by ourselves.

RISE SISTER RISE

What is your relationship with other women?

Do you trust them? If not, what caused this mistrust?

What does this part of you need to hear?

Δ

WHO TRIGGERS YOU?

Do not dismiss or avoid the women who rub you up the wrong way. The ones who piss you off. The ones who offend you. The ones you mistrust. For somewhere in their spikiness or forwardness or weakness or aggressiveness or gorgeousness or arrogance or inexperience they possess a gift. A gift that, through delving deep enough, contains a gem so precious and powerful that you will one day soon, praise the day they came into your view.

Who triggers you? Who annoys you? Who intimidates you? Who rubs you up the wrong way? Who is too harsh? Too soft? Too egotistical? Too plain? Who makes you turn into a crazy lady? Who disgusts you? Who do you find a pain? Who brings out your inner banshee? Who do you resent most of all? Who makes you feel inadequate? Who overlooks you? Who saddens you? Who do you wish you never ever met?

RISE SISTER RISE

Who triggers you?

What do they trigger in you?

What do you allow this to say about you?

What wound are they inviting you to heal?

What dormant power are they inviting you to reclaim?

△

WHY JEALOUSY IS A GOOD THING

'It's a sign of insecurity to be hostile with the unfamiliar.'
ANAÏS NIN

Jealousy is a totally normal human emotion that causes a separation between She and Me. But if you allow yourself to be present with it for long enough, you may just find that your jealousy can be a valuable tool when it comes to getting clear with what you are here to contribute.

Jealousy triggers the part of us that sees ourselves as separate. So when we discover that someone else has something we want, we believe that because they have it, it means we cannot. Jealousy shines a light on what we deeply desire for ourselves. A creation you haven't gotten around to making happen, an experience you have been yearning to have, a decision you have been avoiding making.

Our jealous pangs can hint at the ways we have been keeping ourselves small. They can also reveal the ways we are looking at external approval as a sense of validation. When your jealousy is triggered, it could be a big fat sign pointing to where you should be investing your energy and what the Universe is wanting to create with YOU.

RISE SISTER RISE

Who are you jealous of?

Why are you jealous of them?

How can you allow yourself to create or receive
your own unique version of that for yourself?

△
THERE IS NO COMPETITION

The more time you spend comparing yourself to others the more similar your work will become and the further away you will get from the work you came here to do. Creating your life's work takes time. Don't rush it. Resist the need to rush to market, the creations that your soul has to share are much more potent if you give them ample time to bloom. Don't rush straight into execution. Spend time hanging out with the energies that are beckoning to dance through you.

I have a friend with a very similar purpose and message to mine. We discovered each other a couple of years ago after each of us spending several years getting to that point. The way we express our work in the world is very different because, like many people, we are very different. Our personalities, style, stories, and experiences deliver the same message and at times same energies in very different ways.

We are not in competition; we are sisters on a similar journey. I see how committed she is to her spiritual practice and life's work and have found a treasured kinship in this commonality, as I have with other women who are walking a similar path. This is not to say that we must all be BFFs with everyone. That is just not possible. I can spot my sisters a mile off. It has nothing to do with what they are saying, rather what their energy is communicating. There is a soul recognition, like a subtle nod to someone that is familiar. The same goes for those whose life or message is not in alignment. Those who have gotten so excited to do the work that they have modeled themselves on the person (people) who inspired them, creating the same thing instead of their own unique creation.

Being inspired is wonderful and necessary for art and creativity to be born. However, after we get steady walking on our own, the real sign of a true artist or writer or teacher or creator is their ability to use that inspiration to delve deep within themselves and deep into their devotion to create what is theirs to create. Not a tweaked version of someone else's creations or style.

RISE SISTER RISE

Who have you been seeing as competition
who could be a companion?

How is your need to push or be seen causing
you to be slightly inauthentic?

Δ

RAISE THEM UP DON'T CUT THEM DOWN

Raise them up don't cut them down.

Success is not a limited resource.

Raise them up don't cut them down.

Your power cannot be taken, if you draw it from deep within.

Raise them up don't cut them down.

Your rising does not require someone else to fall.

Raise them up don't cut them down.

△

DON'T PUT ANOTHER ON A PEDESTAL

We are all human. Magnificent and imperfect all at the same time. No matter how much you admire someone, don't put them on a pedestal. For as soon as you do, you raise them up higher than you. And so in order for you some day to join them, that person will have to fall.

Instead of raising them up to giddying heights, start by recognizing that the thing you see in them is likely to be the same thing that is rising in you. What is in you may only be a seed but it is still there, and seeds were created to rise toward the light. Offer deep respect, honor, and admiration, but don't hold them higher than you. Use them as your signal from the Universe of what is ready to rise in you.

RISE SISTER RISE

Who have you been holding up on a pedestal?

What is it in them that is also rising in you?

△

ACKNOWLEDGE YOUR SISTERS

'If we each have a torch, there's a lot more light.'
GLORIA STEINEM

Ever since our souls chose to come to Earth and be in this human body separate from everyone else, we have been battling with the feeling of being left all alone. I'm not talking about your ability to be alone, I'm talking about being separate. What I have come to know to be true is that all of us fear being cast aside.

My friend Amy Firth and I saw Oprah speak in Sydney. Our favorite moment was when she revealed that after interviewing thousands and thousands of people, from Tina Turner to Obama, from Beyonce to Dr. Phil, the moment they all stopped filming they just wanted to know: 'Was that alright?'

We are all looking for validation, acceptance, that what we have to offer is of some value to the world. That the other person truly sees what we have to offer.

It doesn't matter whether you are just starting out or have been rising for over 30 years, deep down we all yearn to be acknowledged for doing our best. Your witnessing of that is both free and priceless. As you offer this valuable gift you will discover that the richness returns to you.

RISE SISTER RISE

Acknowledge someone in your life for the value that
they are offering to the world. Especially the ones
that you think wouldn't need to hear it. For you
may just find that they yearn for it the most.

△

YOUR INNER CIRCLE

*'Lots of people will want to ride with you in the
limo, but what you want is someone who will
take the bus when your limo breaks down.'*
OPRAH

While every woman is deserving of your respect, you are not meant to be friends with everyone. Some women will love you, others will not. And that is OK! Don't spend your days trying to gain everyone's approval. You'll never succeed. Worse: You'll miss out on creating deep connections with those who were born to walk alongside you. A potent posse or coven is much better than 100 people posting 'happy birthday' on your Facebook wall. Every woman should have an inner circle that she keeps sacred. Made up of women that they carefully choose.

**Inviting women into your inner circle is a
sacred act; be mindful of who you invite in.**

Women who will catch us when we fall. Women who hold us when we lay our shame out on the table (something we all should do regularly). Women who love you when you are struggling to love yourself. Women who can say the most brutally honest thing while tenderly cradling your heart. Women who know that just because you feel a certain way today, doesn't mean that is how you will feel a year from now.

Your soul recognizes a sister in an instant. The years do not matter. Neither does location. You can be held from all corners of the Earth. Some of my sisters live on the opposite side of the planet, some I have only met in human flesh once or twice. Years have nothing on lifetimes.

RISE SISTER RISE

Who is in your inner circle of sisters?

Do you need to call any more in?

YOUR SUPPORT TEAM

Rising ain't easy. No one can do it alone. We all need our team of people beside us cheering us on.

Your support team consists of all of the people who have ever believed in you. Those who have your back. Those who have encouraged you. Past, present, and even future, call upon them all. Call on your sisters, your brothers, your teachers, and your friends. Call upon your beloved peers, your followers, that complimentary journalist, and that friendly stranger on the bus.

Each time before I go on stage or sit down to write, I call upon all of these people to stand beside me. Encouraging me on when I begin to doubt myself, to strengthen me when I'm feeling weak. If I'm really nervous, I'll send out a message to my nearest and dearest requesting that they send their good vibes and hold me at that point in time. You don't need to go at it alone. Call upon and receive the support of all the people in your life who have ever given it. Swim in their support.

RISE SISTER RISE

Write a list of all of the people in the world who have ever supported you. Past and present, in ways big and small, recall them all. Anyone who has ever been in your corner. Add my name while you're at it. And so the next time you are called to rise, you can call upon this awesome team for support.

△

THE WOMEN WHO CAME BEFORE YOU

When certain people die, wisdom keepers, light bearers, all that they held is suddenly dispersed among many. Like a star exploding leaving sparks in each of our hearts. You don't need to know the person to feel the impact of their spirit transitioning from physical form, for it to encourage your own expansion.

I felt this deeply when Maya Angelou went home. An ancient custodian of feminine wisdom leaving the planet, while her light ignited our hearts a little more than before. A life force both divine and human that cannot be extinguished. I felt the same the day my friend Blair Milan died.

A kind of passing of the baton can also occur when we lose significant people in our lives that have been holding the light for others. As if their seeds of wisdom, light, and devotion are transmitted in their passing. This was the case for my friend Amy Firth the day that her nan, Moira, journeyed back into the realm of spirit. She had been one of the first female ministers in Australia, and Amy had always had a special bond with her courageous and adventurous nan. More like sisters than grandmother and granddaughter. Both black sheep in a way, neither able to settle to a normal caged life. Both knowing they were here to answer a greater call. Wild women with whopping hearts and a love for the messy things in life.

When Amy told me the news of her nan's sudden passing, I could feel that what had seemingly been extinguished in Moira had been relit in Amy, unable to shake the feeling that in her passing she had passed the torch to Amy. Preparing Amy to continue walking the path she had courageously paved. And that Amy's life was never going to be the same. Back in Australia I attended Moira's memorial at the Uniting Church where she ministered. In her place at the pulpit, Amy gave her first eulogy. Three years on I am to attend Amy's ordination when she will become an Interfaith Minister.

There are many light keepers and wisdom holders who have trodden the path before you. And, in some cases, for you. Both those you know and those you didn't even know existed. Women whose dedication to both spirit and humanity is then gifted and passed on like a luminous torch.

You stand on the shoulders of thousands upon thousands of magnificent women. Those who have come before and those who will continue to come again. And just as we are each made of stardust, we are also made of each of them.

#RISESISTERRISE MANTRA

I call upon the resilience, strength, and support
of all the women who have walked before me.
With them beside me, I never walk alone.

RISE SISTER RISE

Who have you lost (whether you knew them in
person or not) that ignited a light in you?

What women who came before you,
have paved the path for you?

Call upon them.

Behind every risen woman
is a group of women who

p
a
v
e
d

t
h
e

w
a
y
.

△

WE ARE THE MARGUERITES, THE MAGDALENES, AND THE CRONES

We are the ones who stood alone to pave the path before you. We are the ones who fought for what so many of you are now able to take for granted. The ones who remember a time before the hiding and the struggle. A time when all women were deeply respected and unafraid to share their birth rite. Who knew their worth, embodied their power, and deeply trusted their intuition. Who drew their strength from their very core and shared their magic freely.

Our deepest wish is that you recognize and use the gifts that so plentifully abound. That you unveil your medicine and not resist sharing it with the world. To remember the pact from long ago. To continue the path that we started so long ago.

The time has come for one and all to take their place and rise. To step forward, to rise on up and walk the path just like we planned. The veil of silence has been lifted. Your message is your life. Now free your voice, unbind your power, forge a new path, create a new model, and rise.

The time is now. You are on due course. Let's unite and remember what we started so long ago.

RISE SISTER RISE

How are you being called to step up and rise?

Varied in body.

Ancient in soul.

Together they called in the future.

Just like they always planned.

Part VI

DOING THE WORK

She didn't choose Her path
As much as it chose Her.

△

WHAT IS RISING IN YOU?

What is rising in you? What is bubbling up? What is ready to overspill?

What is impatiently tugging, nagging, bursting to be birthed?

What's demanding your attention? What's crying out late at night? What is longing to be ushered into form?

A child, a book, a creation, a reclamation of something true.

That, all of that, is what is rising in you.

When we connect with the boundless well of our heart, we connect the inspiration of Divine Mother with the power of Divine Father. Inspiration and creation merge with surrender and daily action.

**Give in to the bubbling, surrender to
the swelling, show up every day.**

For when you express what is in your soul, or rather let what is in your soul express itself through you, you effortlessly dive into the current of a life in alignment. And when you live a life in alignment, your unique presence alone contributes to the healing of the planet. And when you draw your last breath, you do so knowing that you being here has left the planet a little more harmonious than it was before.

RISE SISTER RISE

What is rising in you?

△

RISING FEMININE ARCHETYPES

Through working with thousands of women devoted to Lightworking and the rising of the feminine, I began to see a pattern that informed their personalities and the work that they came here to do. This pattern can be separated into the following seven Rising Feminine Archetypes.

While each of us has access to all of these archetypes, I've found that we tend to have a primary, and sometimes secondary, one as our baseline. We can deepen our understanding of ourselves and our calling through the lens of the archetype. Furthermore, as we possess each of these archetypes on some level, we can call upon each of them as a form of inner council (as you would spirit guides or angels).

Read the descriptions below and see which archetype you resonate with most.

The High Priestess (crown chakra)

A female priest of sorts, she is a mystical bridge between the worlds, channeling information, creating beauty and harmony through her work. High Priestesses are leaders of light in the world. The High Priestess is so devoted to her purpose and her work that she may find it difficult to put her personal life or relationship first, as she feels such a duty to her work. She is wed to the divine. High Priestesses of times past were responsible for offering ritual so that the sun could rise and set. Linked to Virgo and Venus, she feels a great responsibility to ensure everything is perfect and that there is beauty, balance, and harmony in the world. Prayer and Devotion are her middle names. High Priestesses often remember why they incarnated from a very early age and her holy work is always her priority. But in order to serve in a sustainable way the High Priestess must first learn to serve herself.

The Seer (third-eye chakra)

The Seer has an astute intuition and an ability to see things others cannot. Like the High Priestess she is a bridge between the seen and unseen worlds. Highly sensitive, psychic, and visionary, with an intensity she journeys deep and to often dark places and is not afraid (or has learned not to be afraid) to face the shadows. Her clear vision allows her to cut through any sort of inauthenticity. She often has a tendency to say it like it is, and her truth speaking can sometimes trigger those who are used to a world in which things are seen but not spoken about.

The Storyteller/Artist (throat chakra)

The Storyteller/Artist is here to express and be heard, to share her stories, opinions, ideas, and creations with the world. She makes a wonderful speaker, writer, performer, and teacher. Rarely lost for words, the passing down of information is what she came here to do. She receives so many ideas that it is important that she finds a channel for her creations to be funneled into and shared. The storyteller is at her most powerful when she is focused on passing down wisdom rather than being the student who feels unprepared.

The Healer (heart chakra)

The Healer feels things very deeply. She is unconditional with her loving. A natural empath, she is highly sensitive to her environment. She has a huge heart and a tender capacity to relate and hold others during their darkest hours. She sees the wholeness of all people and is not quick to judge; you can say just about anything to a healer and be accepted with love. She can see the good and light in all. The Healer needs to remember that in order to heal others she must first tend to her own healing, and that it is OK to receive abundance for her work.

The Warrior/Wild Woman (solar plexus chakra)

The Warrior/Wild Woman is fierce! She is the game changer and the activist of the world. She possesses Joan of Arc-like courage, and is not afraid to make a stand and go where others are afraid. Often speaking out about issues she feels need to change, the Warrior/Wild Woman is here to bring about justice. You cannot restrain her. She is boundless. The Warrior/Wild Woman needs to remember to fight for what she is FOR rather than resist what she is AGAINST.

The Natural Witch/Medicine Woman (sacral chakra)

Like the Seer, the Natural Witch/Medicine Woman has the capacity to journey into the shadows in order to find the light. Through history she has been misunderstood and at times mistreated, and so may feel fear or defensiveness around being accepted by the world. At essence the Natural Witch is one with the Earth. Connected to the cyclic nature of life, she is in tune with the seasons, animals, the Moon, and the body. A guardian of the Earth, she sees the sacredness of all life and knows how to use the elements to create magic for herself and others.

The Earth Mother/Midwife (root chakra)

The Earth Mother is the midwife of the world. She is here to usher in the new through encouraging, supporting, and assisting others. Often very grounded, the Earth Mother is here to birth the potential of the world. She possesses a mother-bear-like energy when she needs to protect what is being birthed. Highly compassionate and very hands on, she makes a wonderful host, loves caring for others, and being in a relationship and surrounded by people.

RISE SISTER RISE

What do you think is your primary Rising Feminine Archetype?

△
NEW WORLD RISING BIRTHED BY YOU

We are the creators and change-makers birthing a new world. We are the artists and midwives for this new consciousness that is beckoning to be brought forth. Catalysts of change, ushering in a new age. Our CEO: She.

We are the women birthing and nurturing new ideas and ways of being on behalf of the planet. Voicing things that have for too long been left unsaid. Remembering long-forgotten wisdom. Bringing the fierce feminine back for good.

And while that all sounds idealistic and lovely, this process ain't easy. But birth never is.

So the next time you're doubting yourself think of the miracle of birth, that big round head, neck and shoulders pushing its way through a seemingly much smaller space. For what you are called to do is likely as natural and excruciating and rewarding and necessary and exhilarating and impossible and miraculous as that.

No matter what you are birthing, the process is always going to be full of contractions and tension and 'I can't do this' and 'OMGing.' We must groan and moan and scream and grind and kick and breeeeeeathe our way through it.

And while there are times that we think we simply cannot, if you allow it, something guttural and sacred then takes over. The stubborn, crazy amazing process of Life.

Every time we are called to grow and change, we are birthing ourselves. This process is never ending once you are on the path of She. This is not the time to keep your moans quiet; let your pain roar. For when you do, you transmute this pain into power. Use it. Use it all.

No matter whether you are birthing a creation or being birthed yourself, you are going to need a birthing team. Those who are on your side, at your beck and call, wiping your brow and encouraging you to go on when you doubt the immensity of the thing that you have taken on. Midwives and cheerleaders who can see the light at the end of the tunnel and above all else, remind you that you already know when to breathe and when to push...

When you devote your life to being of service, you have She on your team.

RISE SISTER RISE

What are you birthing or called to birth right now (it can be yourself if it's not a project or specific thing)?

Who are your team of midwives who can help you birth this project or a transformation of yourself into the world (e.g. friends, peers, coach, healer)?

Are there any more you need to call in?
Assemble your birthing team.

△

LET THE UNIVERSE USE YOU

The quickest way to fall into flow with the Universe is to allow Her to use you. Being of service is merely being in flow with the Universe.

Anything any human has done you can do too. Which means that Oprah or Lady Gaga or Beyonce or Prince or Amma or whoever you admire is no more special than you. They are no less special than you either. What we see as 'special' is their ability to work WITH the Universe and allow their true nature to be revealed. They have learned how to say yes to the highest potential in store for them, rather than trying to scheme it up themselves. They have surrendered and invited the Universe to work through them. Perhaps they are better at surrendering but they are no more special or unique than you.

We waste so much time trying to strategize what we should do next, overthinking every move. I am blown away at how many people I admire say, when questioned, 'It all just kind of happened.' THAT is flow. THAT is service. THAT is surrendering to what is rising in you, because...

What is rising in you IS what the Universe has in store for you.

Your only job is to continue to commune and show up every day saying YES, YES, YES. If we bow to this organizing principle and surrender to it over and over again, our path and highest possible potential will not just be shown, it will be made real. But if we wait for the roadmap before we trust or move, we risk remaining stuck.

The Universe, this intelligent force, wants you to succeed. It wants you to flow with it, for when you flow with it you are moving in service to it. So to be of service is really to turn to the Universe and say, I will not resist or rely on my separate strength any longer. I am now willing to surrender to She and all that is.

The two forms of spiritual practice that I have found most helpful for falling into flow with the Universe are Light Sourcing (*see below*) and Intuitive Nature Walking (*see page 101*).

Light Sourcing is a form of meditation, which connects you to, and aligns you with, the unlimited light Source of the Universe, so that you flow with it and in a state to receive all of the things that are ready to come to you. To allow your cells to get into alignment with the same power that governs the spinning of the planets, the tides, the moon, our monthly cycle, all of it. Within a month of doing this practice my life began to change. Within a year of doing this practice all that I deeply yearned for was my reality – things didn't work out how I expected them to, they worked out better. For I was flowing with Life so Life was flowing with me.

Another tool to get you in the flow of service and surrender to the Universe is the following prayer from *A Course In Miracles*. I say it several times every day:

I am here to be truly helpful.
I'm here to represent that which sent me.
I do not have to think about what to say or do
Because that which sent me will direct me.
I'm happy just to be here.
Knowing that all grace is within me.
I will be healed as I let the healing happen through me.

RISE SISTER RISE

Download the free Light Sourcing Meditation at www. risesisterrise.com. Make it a daily practice for 21 days and notice how the Universe bends toward you.

$\triangle$

BE A CLEAR CHANNEL

If you long to be of service, bow down and say the following prayer:

**'Please use me. Please lead me.
Please show me the way.'**

Then run for cover.

Because the moment you utter those words, the Universe conspires to uproot and stir up and shine a floodlight on absolutely everything that stands in the way of you being a crystal-clear channel for the divine to work through.

A calling is not something you choose, but something that chooses you. It grabs you by the soul strings and won't let you rest until you answer it. Sometimes answering your calling is one of the most difficult things you will ever do, but the only thing more difficult than answering it is not answering it. However, in answering it, in surrendering to it, you will also experience the sheer daily bliss of being able to devote your life to having the Universe shine its light through you. And as far as I am concerned, there is no better feeling than that. And that is not just reserved for a special few, rather it is available for us all.

#RISESISTERRISE MANTRA

Please use me. Please lead me. Please show me the way.

Δ

A PRAYER FOR TIMES OF REMEMBERING

May every soul hear the whispers of times forgotten.

May every body be unleashed and unchained.

May each vow of silence be dissolved for ever more.

May all seeds of light planted sprout, rise and bloom.

May sacred lands continue to sing songs of remembering.

May every human heart beat in harmony with the rhythm of Life.

And so it is. And so it is. And so it is.

△
IT'S NOT YOUR JOB TO SAVE THE WORLD

You are not here to save the world. No matter what kind of mission you have, the only person you are here to save is yourself.

Moreover, the ONLY person you CAN save is yourself.

In working your light, you may inspire others to work theirs. But you must not take credit for it as they will have done the work, not you.

It's not your job to save or change anyone. There is nothing more annoying than someone who is pushing their spirituality, consciousness, opinions or anything else for that matter on another without invitation. It doesn't matter if it's meditation, yoga, past lives, working with your chakras, raising your vibration, your choice to be a vegetarian, or the power of prayer. Do not give spirituality a bad name by spreading the good news or pushing your beliefs on another without invitation. This is what patriarchy has been about: *'Do as I say,'* 'Obey,' 'This is the only way,' 'Follow the leader'... We've had enough of that.

Instead let your life be the message. Let your devotion be felt, not pushed down someone's throat. Live in alignment with your spirit and let others choose to do the same. Even if you think you might know better – especially if you think you know better – it's none of your business.

If they inquire, then by all means offer it all up on a beautiful platter, but ask permission first. Each soul that resonates with your vibration has all that they need to awaken. But the only one who can choose it is them. And it is a choice.

**Don't push your consciousness on another.
Vibration speaks louder than words.**

Living in accordance to your own light will work way harder than your words ever could. Let your vibration do the talking. It's not your job to save the world.

RISE SISTER RISE

Who in your life are you trying to save or convince?

How can you let your vibration do the talking instead?

THE AGE OF THE STRUGGLING ARTIST AND HEALER IS OVER

If you are living a life in alignment and devoted to being of service then the gifts that you share are priceless. Don't think that just because you would do them for free, you should. If you are called to spend your life offering up these gifts, you deserve to be rewarded for them. The age of the struggling artist and wounded healer is over.

When you are doing the work that is yours, when you are living in congruence, when you are courageously answering what is truly rising in you, you are helping the planet move back into harmony. In other words, you are moving as one with the Universe rather than resisting it.

If everyone on the planet realigned their lives and did the work that is right for them, we would have a very different world. That world is drawing near.

Most artists, intuitives, healers, mystics, Lightworkers, etc., go through a stage of feeling uncomfortable about asking for payment for what they love doing. However, if we are going to serve as many people as possible, we need to be able to look after ourselves and thrive. If we don't give ourselves the nourishment we need in order to do the work in a sustainable way, we are cheating those we are here to serve.

As my audience grows, the amount of devotional practice and self-care that I need to do does too. There is so much we still don't know about the energetic effects of technology, such as social media and creations being out there with the masses. We must protect our energy by cutting off from our creations once we release them into the world and then give ourselves whatever we need to support our wellbeing. The work you are here to share is priceless. And for most artists and healers and the like, the work is done in subtle ways. That is, the one hour of your time that you are offering, is, energetically speaking, more than one hour of your time.

When I first started my business I was struggling at the concept of asking my clients who were in personal crisis to pay me. I had no boundaries, answering emails late at night and giving more of my time than agreed. I'll never forget the advice my teacher Sonia gave me, 'Be like a butcher.'

If someone buys six sausages from a butcher they don't give you eight; they don't give their sausages away for free or at a discounted price; they don't answer emails at 10 p.m. at night; they don't spend hours questioning whether they are good enough; they just show up and sell their sausages like a normal person shows up to work. Because that's their job, they're a butcher. Show up, do your job to the best of your ability and cut off when you clock off so that you can do it again the next day. Simple.

RISE SISTER RISE

Is there any part of you that believes you should not be extremely abundant for doing what you love or helping others?

What is one hour of your time worth to you?

In order to do the work you are here to do, what self-care do you need to do every week?

△

YOU CAN'T BUY DEVOTION

Devotion can only be gathered by showing up over and over again with intention. In the Age of Light devotion is everything. What are you showing up to with devotion every day?

As a feminine leader of this new age your devotion is what will be felt. People will be able to sense if you are in it for you and your own gain or if you are in it for them, for we, for thee.

When you live your life in devotion you live your life in ultimate service. When we show up to our devotional practice, we are aligned to service and authenticity instantly. When we are aligned, that which is meant for us starts moving toward us like a magnet. You go from my will to thy will. You go from trying to control, manipulate, and strive, to surrendering in full. Your daily devotional practice gives our lives rhythm, a beat to live to.

In order to live a life of devotion, a devotional practice is imperative, whether that is meditation, chanting, Light Sourcing, yoga, prayer, or something else. The more you show up to your devotional practice the more you will be held. The more you are held, the easier the devotion becomes. You are carried. For you are not doing it for an outcome, rather your whole life becomes one big moving prayer.

RISE SISTER RISE

What does your daily devotional practice consist of currently?

Are you being called to up the ante?

Every step She took in devotion
The Universe took ten.

△

THE CREATIVE PROCESS IS
AN ACT OF FAITH

There's no difference between creativity and spirit. There are ideas waiting to be thought up, creations beckoning to be birthed, movies bursting to be filmed, words yearning to be written, consciousness ready to rise. And they're all looking for artists to birth them. The creative process is an act of faith. There's no certainty. It's in a way a miracle and in a way completely natural. Just like birth.

As artists and creators, our job is to listen with our heart and report back what we hear, feel and see. Living the life of a creative requires a special kind of belief. The creative process itself is the ultimate act of faith. What was once nothing all of a sudden becomes something. The miracle of birth. Receiving an idea or concept is one thing, ushering it into the world is something else. The only thing that is linear about the creative process is that it requires that we religiously show up and nurture our craft, just as a mother does her child. Through the highs and the lows. The rest is one great big leap of faith. Faith in your ability to hear the whispers when they come. Faith in being able to show up to be a vehicle, regardless of what comes through you. Faith in the fact that your muse will never leave you. Faith that all of the pieces will somehow come together.

#RISESISTERRISE MANTRA

I show up every day and allow the
Universe to create through me.

RISE SISTER RISE

What courageous creations are yearning to be birthed by you?

What do they need in order for you to birth them?

△

KEEPING YOUR WORK AND CREATIONS POTENT

A fracturing of energy occurs when you attempt to do too many things at once. When you put your attention in too many places, when you try to spin too many plates. I'm not just talking about the energy required to do the task in the moment, rather the energy that the creation contains and holds itself so it can survive in the world without you once you set it free.

In this age of multitasking and comparison the potency of our energy runs the risk of getting fractured. And so while we may end up with a lot of opportunities or blog posts or projects, the potency is often being spread too thin.

I have spent a lot of my life doing too much. Trying to fit it all in. Some of it driven by a fear of not wanting to miss out, wanting to keep up or stay ahead, but to be honest, it's mostly because there is just so much that I want to experience and create. So I've said, 'Yes, yes, yes,' when often in hindsight I should have been saying, 'Yes, no, no.'

I now split my year into four three-month periods. For each of these three-month periods, I am only allowed to focus on one thing, one creation that I am most called to bring into the world. At present my focus is writing this book. Any new opportunity that pops up during that period, no matter how awesome it is, I ask myself the following question, 'If I say yes to this opportunity, will I run the risk of not getting this creation done to the best of my ability with the potency of my energy in the time frame I have set out before me?' If the answer is 'Yes,' my response is 'No thank you.'

RISE SISTER RISE

How are you spreading yourself too thin?

What creation do you most want to bring into the world with potency in the next three months?

What could get in the way of giving it your full attention?

△

CREATE WHAT IS YOURS TO CREATE

Don't focus on quantity, instead focus on quality. You are here to create what is yours to create. There is no rush. There is no competition. When you try to fill the space of your life and the space of the world around you with stuff in an effort to keep up with those around you, you deny the world the special shade of light that you came here to share.

So water your garden, fan your flames, and keep your focus inward. Let your creations be your medicine then share that medicine with the world. When you keep your focus on what is yours to create, you do not need to look left or right.

That way, you will find that what you came here to do is the very thing that you would actually choose to do. You will find that your medicine is the very thing that nourishes and fuels you and others. Which means that your creations will never ever run dry.

RISE SISTER RISE

What is truly yours to create?

△

SELF-CARE BEFORE SERVICE (NO MORE WOUNDED HEALERS)

The days of the wounded healer who is busy taking care of everyone else but herself must stop. If you want to do this work you must be sustainable. Remember: A life's work, not a season. It is imperative that you give yourself the nourishment that you need. Better steady and sustainable rather than quick and un-sustaining.

When you are committed to your rising, you must honor the healing that needs to take place within you. And sometimes the most productive thing to do is to stop everything and tend to that. To process that. To embody that. To know the subtle difference between when to make it happen and when to let it happen.

Do not resist your body's self-care needs. You are being called to birth this new world, but in order to do so you must put your needs and tend to your own inner well as a priority. You are no use to anyone exhausted and parched. One can only share what she has in plenty. We must be ferocious in ensuring we tend to our own self-care before service. We must be sustainable in order to rise and bring about consistent change.

RISE SISTER RISE

How am I putting others' healing ahead of my own?

What am I being called to heal in me?

BELOVED MOTHER MARY

Thank you for helping me decipher

When to be of service to the world

And when to be of service to myself.

And so it is. And so it is. And so it is.

△

BE OK WITH WHERE YOU ARE

You do not need to be anywhere other than where you are right now. You do not need anything other than what you have right now. Don't spend your time striving to be somewhere else. Instead, focus on where you are. Life is always leading us, but we cannot hear Her call if we do not ground ourselves in the current moment.

If you are thinking of the future so much, by the time you get to it, you'll be thinking of another future. So all of the hard work and sacrifices you are putting into getting to the future won't be enjoyed because the bar will always be rising. Celebrate your creations when they happen. Take a moment to breathe and truly enjoy them.

**What good is a creation or a success if you
do not allow yourself to enjoy it?**

Don't keep pushing the finishing line back mid-run. Be OK with where you are. For where you are is where Life is. And if you are constantly looking at the next thing you are not truly flowing with Life.

If where you are is uncomfortable, be in the uncomfortable. If where you are is exciting, be with the excitement. If where you are is in grief, be with the grief. All moments will end. Don't miss them or drag them out by not being present with where you are today.

RISE SISTER RISE

How are you striving to be somewhere
other than where you are right now?

How can you be more OK with where you are today?

△

CREATE FOR YOU AND YOU ALONE

Once you birth your creations in the world they are no longer yours. Just like a child that you have nurtured into adulthood, your creations have a life, seasons and a purpose of their own. And as hard as it may be, you must let them fulfill it on their own.

It doesn't matter what people think or what happens once you release them into the world. All that matters is that what started as a seed has been set free to be whatever it was always destined to be. You have no control over how people will receive your creations. But never forget:

**Far more people regret not creating
than they do actually creating.**

The tighter you cling and hold on to your creations, the harder it will be ever to create again. Don't read the reviews, don't look at the sales figures. Just know that you gave it all that you could, celebrate, take a break, and get ready to create something new.

The best artists and creators are the ones that would do what they do regardless of the outcome. They are not attached to what their creations will bring them. And much more focused on the magic of creation.

Once you start out it's easy to look at your heroine and be attached to manifesting what their creations have attracted. To fall in love with the life rather than the work. Once you start getting successful it's also easy to expect all that comes with it. However, as artists and creators this is a slippery slope, for the bar will always continue to rise and fall. Your best work may be rejected and overlooked. Your worst may be celebrated.

Neither is your business. Having your sense of worth or success attached to it would be a big mistake. Huge.

Instead, show up and create because that is what you were put on this planet to do. Show up and create because you love the smell of paint. Show up and create because symmetrical websites make you feel more balanced yourself. Show up and create because it lights you up more than anything else. Show up and create because sharing your story calms your inner crazy.

If you are doing anything for the recognition or the validation or the fame then you are doing it for the wrong reason. It is your separateness that is seeking the validation and this is a thirst that can never be quenched. Either stop what you are doing or find a way to reframe.

Every time you show up to create, you are devoting yourself to something bigger. Every time you create you get to know yourself a little bit better. A call is something that chooses us. Rising to answer it is a sacred thing. It is not about you. You are a mere note in the Universe's song. You may get recognition for doing what is yours to do, or, you might be called to do it with no recognition at all. One is not better than the other. Focus on playing your note as best you can and forget about how many people are listening, how many people think you sound sweet and how many people think you sound off. Play your note anyway and allow the breath of the Universe to exhale through you. In doing so you will discover that letting your self be sung is reward enough. If not, time to find something else.

Find a way to breathe life into your bravest creations today. When you put your creations out there you run the risk of being judged. And the better and more cutting-edge the work, the more it will be judged – by those who are not ready for it or misunderstand it or project their stuff onto it. All of that is out of your hands. So if you want to be successful or just a great artist, get ready to be judged. The more successful you are, or unique or courageous you are with your creations, the more people will project their stuff onto you. Their opinions actually have nothing to do with you. Everything in life is subjective, most of all something as intangible as art.

When I worked in advertising I was so attached to the outcome of what my bosses thought of my creations. I would present idea after idea, only to be devastated when they were rejected – scrunched up and thrown in the trash in front of me. My response to one particular Creative Director continued this way until I finally learned to be detached from his opinion and instead enjoy the process of creating.

The best teachers, like artists, are OK with not being liked. They create because they love creating.

RISE SISTER RISE

What creations are you being called to create right now?

Why do you want to create them?

Whose approval are you attached to?

What outcome are you attached to?

△

DON'T BELIEVE YOUR OWN PR

*'I have already settled it for myself so flattery and
criticism go down the same drain and I am quite free.'*
GEORGIA O'KEEFFE

'Don't believe your own PR.' That's what my teacher Sonia told me at
the beginning of my career. Thank God for good teachers.

Don't let someone else's opinion of you be any way linked to your
opinion of yourself. If you attach your identity and worth to what others
say, feel, do, or think, you are setting yourself up for a hefty fall. And
eventually, you will fall, that is a guarantee. For if you are attached to the
good things people say about you, you are attached to the bad things
they say about you too.

When I first started doing intuitive readings I was attached to the
outcome of them going really well, of getting it right, of creating a
considerable shift in my clients. My need for validation was getting in
the way of simply being a clear channel. My identity as an intuitive was
attached to other people's opinions. I wanted so much to help others
that I attached my sense of value to what other people thought.

At first this worked fine, because the feedback was great. I'd read
the emails of flowing feedback and felt so good about my work. But
eventually, after more than one hundred happy clients I had one who
was not. This person would turn out to be one of my biggest teachers.
In one fell swoop my sense of self and value as an intuitive guide was
shattered. It took some serious uprooting, but eventually I found a way
to draw my sense of self unwaveringly from within.

This is extremely difficult in a world of likes, retweets, comparison, and followers. How often do you reach for your phone and get a little rush from how much validation the outside world has given you? It is often said that fame and approval are the most addictive drugs of all.

The lovers are out there and the haters are too. Let it all be background noise to the voice that bellows from deep within you. The more you do what you are called to do, the more haters will appear. If you believe your fans then you will believe your critics too. But, if you draw your sense of self from deep within, then you can just get on with doing the work that you were put on this planet to do.

RISE SISTER RISE

Are you attached to what people think of you (good or bad)?

How can you draw your sense of self from within?

△

YOU DON'T NEED SAVING

Your soul can be calling you to rise up every moment of every day but without daily action all of those calls are useless. In fact, without daily action those daily calls are frustrating! If you are going to listen to the calls of your soul you must ACT on them.

We are mostly fifth-dimensional spiritual beings having a third-dimensional human experience. We create our tomorrow by our intentions and actions today. The more in touch with your intuition you are, the easier it is to tune in to future possibilities that are aligning to you.

A common mistake of the highly conscious is that the moment we see the potential outcome – for example a relationship, job, money, etc. – we stop acting, in the belief that because we have had the vision or the confirmation it is coming. But when we receive a vision it is actually the *potential* we are tapping into, not the third-dimensional reality of the manifestation in action. And when it doesn't come, we get frustrated and confused because we were so sure it was coming, which it was, but the moment we assumed it was coming we stopped acting. That is, WE intuited the manifestation (i.e. a job) but the moment we intuited it, we stopped doing what was necessary to ground that thing into physical form (through daily grounded action).

No matter how 'spiritual' or 'intuitive' we are, remember that while we are in our human suits, third-dimensional rules apply. So ground your dreams through daily action. That way, you can ensure that you spend your time actually living your dreams rather than dreaming about them.

As you step closer to what you want, what you want is stepping closer to you.

I meet so many aspiring writers, teachers, and artists who are praying for a lucky break. They've had a vision, or an intuitive told them that they will write a book, and now they are waiting for someone to be their knight in shining armor to open doors and make things happen for them. But in doing this they are putting their power in an external force rather than becoming an energetic match for the thing they want. What's more they are often so attached to the outcome and what it will bring them or say about them that it stops them from actually taking action to create it.

You must make the first steps. Every act you do in devotion to what is rising in you, the closer you get. Perhaps your savior is a business mentor who will take your career to the next level, a publisher that will share your voice, or an agent with connections. Don't wait for some external force to come along before you step up and rise. Start creating it for yourself now.

If you are yearning to be rescued you are giving away your power to the very thing you are trying to call in. You are stating very clearly to the Universe that you need saving, which the Universe registers as NEEDING. Meaning you are NOT READY to receive it or hold it in your field. The longer you stay in this needing and waiting state, the longer you will continue not being a vibrational match for the very thing that you are still waiting for.

If there is something you long for, do it because it lights you up and lose yourself in the doing. Don't wait for the end result before you consider taking the next step. If you don't know how to get to where you are going, start building your own bridge. Your soul is always calling you but without daily action those calls will continue to be calls.

RISE SISTER RISE

What is your soul calling you toward right now?

What simple action can you take to ground your dreams today?

△

LIGHTWORKERS GOTTA WORK

*'Are you here to do the work or are you
just wanting to look good?'*
KYLE GRAY

If you don't embody your work, people will feel it. Whether it is releasing a song, a piece of artwork, teaching, healing, or presenting in a meeting, it is not your words, concepts, or creations that people are drawn to, it is your devotion to it.

Your ability to hold that message, creation, or vibration in your field. Your ability to truly embody and walk your talk.

Your ability to work the light, not just market it.

If you are called to write or teach or create or speak, if you are spending the majority of your time marketing what you do, you are missing the point. It is important that we don't rush into being the biggest and the best, and so dilute the purity and potency of our mission in the process. Marketing should come last. Focus on your devotion to the craft. If your focus is not on your craft you will not find the work that is unique to you or the ancient wisdom that is waiting for you to tap into. Don't be another packaged-up version of what already exists.

**The world needs more artists, seers, medicine women
and healers, midwives, encouragers, visionaries.
It doesn't need more marketers. The world needs
more people working their light, not wearing it.**

Don't get swept up in the latest marketing models and get rich quick/ quick fix schemes. You will likely lose yourself and your audiences' respect in them. The old patriarchal sales models are dissolving away fast. We must forge our own systems and models and as feminine leaders we must do it in a way that is rooted in our feminine cyclic nature.

In a world of information overload, people can tell if you truly embody what you are saying. With the huge surge of people going online now, there is so much grabbing energy. It's exhausting. So many 'clever marketing concepts,' which are basically a regurgitation of the same thing. So much noise that doesn't respect people's inboxes as being sacred spaces. So much lifting of content, almost in a rush to put a stake in the ground. It's exhausting and soul dampening. Don't add to it.

We must become Olympic athletes of devotion. Warriors of our craft. Servants of service. If you are to create a life's work, not a season, you must devote yourself to your craft, not your marketing. Slow and steady always wins in the end. So build your creations with courageous potency, with clear intention, with unwavering focus, and with sacred intent. If you do this, when it comes time to set that creation free into the world, you will have gathered up enough energy so that its own light can fuel it.

RISE SISTER RISE

How are you being called to focus more on your craft?

What are you doing that no longer feels authentic?

What is yours to do?

How can you bring more potency to your work?

△

UNFOLLOW AND LEAD

'Be a voice. Not an echo.'
ALBERT EINSTEIN

Don't flood your newsfeed, or your life for that matter, with people that make you feel like you're not doing enough. So many of my clients suffer from a constant feeling of comparison, competition, inadequacy, and feeling like time is running out.

From our relationships to our business, our creative projects to our friendships, every single thing in our life goes through the four seasons (*see page 105*). We are not meant to be in summer all year round. Everything is circular. The more you try to keep things the same, or keep up with some external measure, the more out of alignment and out of flow you will become.

When someone else is in spring, you may be in winter. Both are important and equally necessary. Don't deny yourself the proper time and nourishment necessary to live through each season.

My client Alex unfollowed 90 percent of those on her social media feed, after noticing that the endless updates of all the awesome things her peers were doing was making her feel inadequate and not trust the season she was in. Soon, extra space was created within her, making way for an idea so groundbreaking and potent that it wouldn't have been possible had she continued playing follow the leader.

So if there are particular people you follow that trigger you into feeling like you are not doing enough or like time is running out, unfollow them with loving grace. The less we consume, the more potent and unique what we have to share will become. Unfollowing can be a sacred act.

RISE SISTER RISE

Who on your newsfeed triggers you?

What do they trigger in you?

Who are you guided to unfollow so you
can more effectively lead?

△
DON'T LOOK BEHIND YOU

If you are constantly looking at what other people are doing, saying, and thinking, you won't create anything significant because your sense of authenticity will be off, and most tragically you will miss the chance to create what is yours to create. Your purpose is different from anyone else's out there. Your purpose is not to be like anyone else. So take that pressure off.

Your purpose is to answer the unique calls of your soul every day. To allow what is falling away to fall. To allow what is rising to rise. No matter how much it excites or scares you. Simple.

Perhaps it was because of the stubborn resolve of my ancestors, but when I was younger I was a really good long-distance runner. My strategy was always to start out strong and establish my lead. It was a combination of wanting to win and wanting to be away from everyone else in nature. I couldn't stand running on top of other people. One race, at the last 800-meter mark we emerged from the bush and around a large field where people were cheering us on to the finish line. I knew the girl in second position was behind me, as I could hear people yelling her name. I made the mistake of looking behind to see where she was. The moment I did that, I could feel the natural flow of energy (Shakti) that was driving me begin to drain out of me. In that moment the race was lost because I was running to her beat rather than running to mine.

The same thing goes for the rest of Life. In my work I follow very few of my peers. While I support their work I don't want to know what they are doing. I don't want their work to influence mine. I want to create what it is that I am here to create, not do what everyone else is doing and lose my own rhythm. I am here to honor the Shakti that is rising in me and express that through my creations and the unique lens I see Life through. We all are.

RISE SISTER RISE

How are you looking behind you?

Are you running to your own beat or someone else's?

Δ

WHAT WOULD MAKE THE BEST CHAPTER?

What would make the best chapter? I ask myself that question a lot. Whenever I'm feeling fearful, when I'm feeling stuck, when I'm not ready to let go, when I am being called to rise but my mind can't quite keep up. Whenever my intuition whispers. Whenever my intuition SHOUTS!

Every person has a life worthy of a book. Every day we have an opportunity to live a new chapter. So the next time you are faced with a decision, ask yourself, 'Which decision would make the best chapter?' Staying at home or going on the life-changing pilgrimage? Asking him out or waiting until he notices that you even exist? Starting your own business or staying in the brain-numbing job that you hate? Telling your mum that you are sorry or pretending that the argument never happened?

You are the author of your story and your life is the book. Make it a bestseller and leap, leap, leap.

RISE SISTER RISE

What decision are you faced with right now that you are afraid of making?

What would make the best chapter?

Δ

RITUAL: PLANT YOUR PRAYERS

May we ground the seeds of light that are in our hearts. May we anchor them into the earth.

Turn to a fresh page in your journal or use this page below to write your heart's deepest prayers for both you and the planet. A love letter to our Beloved Mother and Father Universe. Then rip it out and plant it in the Earth with imaginary seeds of light (even better, plant it with real seeds too).

May all your prayers be planted and bloom forever.

△

YOU HAVE BEEN CALLED

'We are the ones we have been waiting for.'
HOPI WISDOM

The world needs more dreamers, artists, peacekeepers, and awakeners. More change-makers, creators, poets, and rememberers. More visionaries, healers, shamans, and believers.

The world is ready for more empowered, self-assured, potent women. And men who support Her rising. More women who trust their intuition without waver. More women who believe in their own medicine and share it freely. More women who own their power, know their worth and do not dim according to who walks by. More women who aren't afraid to show the world who they really truly are – no matter how magnificent or inconvenient. More women who aren't intimidated by someone else's success. More women who recognize that we are all on the same team. More women who understand the true meaning of sisterhood.

Wise women, wild women, boisterous women, fierce women, idealistic women, Priestess women, medicine women, healing women, stubborn women, expressive women, 'too much' women, unapologetic women, compassionate women, courageous women, encouraging women, opinionated women, confident women, self-assured women, radiant women.

The world is crying out for more mothers – of the Earth, of the unfortunate, of the unprotected, but mostly of themselves. More mothers regardless of birth and babies.

More nature-walkers. More ocean-swimmers. More bridges-of-the-worlds. More spinners-of time-and-space. More weavers of the whispers of the ancients and the concerns of our antecedents. More ceremonies. More ritual. More truth. More meaning.

More women knowing – in their bones and their hearts and their souls – that *it is* possible to heal this wonderful planet by first healing ourselves. More women remembering that they chose to be here at this time. More women finding the courage to rise.

RISE SISTER RISE

How are you being called to rise?

She was a leader of the future.
A protector of the ancient past.

A midwife for what was rising.
Ensuring this incarnation
Was not our last.

△

BEING THE CHANGE BEFORE
IT IS THE NORM

'Living a meaningful life is not a popularity contest.
If what you are saying is always getting applause,
you're probably not yet doing the right stuff.'

MARIANNE WILLIAMSON

Being the change before it is the norm isn't easy. Change-makers change things. They usher in possibilities. Call in new ways of thinking, doing, and being. They birth in the new.

Most people resist change. Because change is scary. Change means letting go. And letting go is painful. You likely know this more than most.

When you come face to face with those who do not understand you, who question you, who are not ready for the message you are bringing in... GOOD! For this is a sure sign you are facing the right direction. Remember, it is not your job to change anyone. Always only yourself.

But don't lose faith. And do not question yourself or your beliefs. For faith is our greatest weapon. Faith that as we rise up, others will too. Faith that in healing ourselves, we are healing the world around us.

Faith that it is never too late. Faith that it is possible for one life to make a difference. Faith that we never do this work alone. Faith that we can create heaven right here on Earth.

I bow down to your willingness to rise at this time. I kiss the path before you. It takes courage and gall to shatter the shackles that once held you, we, She and indeed He captive. For we have come to know our confinement with certainty. This new freedom may bring with it new challenges. If and when it does, know that at every single moment that mysterious force that called you forth is cradling you, loving you, supporting you.

May every new step that we each take, be a step walked for She.

Because...

Alone we are strong. But together, we are fierce.

THE INITIATION

It is with pleasure that we return to offer this initiation.
One that we all have been longing for. And one that
you may remember from a long-ago past.

How long it has been that we have been journeying solo.
But now, at long last, You, We, She have returned.

We welcome you into our sisterhood. Mystics, Healers,
Medicine Women, Guardians of the Earth. Poets, Storytellers,
Healers, Witches, Priestesses of times past. Gathered now
at this sacred moment to birth Her rising once more.

Thank you for returning and being here at this time.
Thank you for doing the work.

It does not matter what has happened and what pain has
occurred. All that matters is that You, We, She have returned.

It is time, dear one, to step forward and claim your throne.
We see you. We recognize you. We remember you.
May you be unbound, unbound, forever unbound.

All ancient secrets are whispered forever in your ears.
All mystic knowing blooms in your heart.
All potent power pumps through your veins.
All abundance bubbles eternal in the wellspring of your womb.

We invite you to step into your ancient knowingness. To be
held by the rememberings and red threads of the Avalon,
Lemuria, Isis, Essene, Mother God, and Magdalene lineages.

To walk tall with the support of those who came
before you and those who will come again.
To unleash your full potent power without waver.
To dance free and unrestrained in your sacred vessel of a body.

To delight in your effortless ability to give birth and create.
To honor the natural rhythms of your body and the planet at large.
To fill up your inner well so that there is
more than enough to go around.
To protect the Great Mother and show others
that heaven is a place on Earth.

In doing this sacred work of the feminine, know that you are never
ever alone. For each step you take in your rising, you also take for She.

May you forever feel the support of your sisters, those
who came before and those who are rising alongside.

Rise Sister Rise.

Today we honor the powerful, wise, compassionate,
ferocious woman that you came here to be. And the
unique medicine that you came here to share.

We kiss the Earth before you as you step into your potency
as a wise, wild woman and Priestess of the High.

The waters ahead may not all be smooth sailing, the
path of rising in times of change never is.
When the seas get choppy know that all of Life is working
with you, not against you, and that you have everything you
need within you to get through any wave, wind or storm.

No matter how dark it gets, may you never stop
seeing the light seeded within it all.

And most of all: May you forever hear Her whisper:

Rise Sister Rise.

RISE SISTER RISE

When your plans and schemes and your hopes
and dreams beg for you to let them go.

Rise Sister Rise.

When the life you have so consciously
created all comes crumbling down.

Rise Sister Rise.

When your soul is heavy and your heart broken in two.

Rise Sister Rise.

When you gave it your best, and it wasn't quite enough.

Rise Sister Rise.

When you've been beaten and defeated
and feel so far away from home.

Rise Sister Rise.

When you find yourself in a million pieces
with no idea which bit goes where.

Rise Sister Rise.

When you have loved and lost. And then lost again.

Rise Sister Rise.

When your wings have been clipped, your spirit
dampened and all you hear is a whisper.

Rise Sister Rise.

When you finally beg mercy to your calling
but have no idea where to start.

Rise Sister Rise.

Rise for you. And rise for me.

For when you rise first

you make the path brighter for She.

Rise for you
Rise for me
When you rise first
You rise for She.

KEEP ON RISING

Thank you for doing this work and sharing these pages with me. It would be my honor for us to continue working together.

Rise Sister Rise: Join the Sisterhood
Join the Rise Sister Rise Sisterhood where you will receive monthly meditations and membership access to the private Facebook circle filled with your fellow rising sisters. Join at www.risesisterrise.com

Online Courses
If you like this book and want to go deeper, check out my online courses at www.rebeccacampbell.me/courses

Rise Sister Rise: Circle, Events, and Retreats
To discover upcoming circles, events and retreats in your city go to www.rebeccacampbell.me/events

Get on the list
Receive free teachings and gifts by signing up for my newsletter at www.rebeccacampbell.me/signup

Stay in touch
www.rebeccacampbell.me

Facebook: rebeccathoughts

Instagram: @rebeccathoughts

Twitter: @rebeccathoughts

ACKNOWLEDGMENTS

To my husband, Craig. Thank you for your support, encouragement, thoughtfulness, confidence, consciousness, and deep respect of the feminine. Marrying you has allowed me to rise from such solid ground. I love and respect you deeply.

To Amy Kiberd, thank you for helping me birth this wild woman into the world and for being such a wonderful midwife every step of the way. I am blessed to have you in my life, both as a friend and an editor. I have no doubt that we arranged it long ago.

To my mother, Julie, and father, Trevor, for giving me so much room and encouragement to rise. You are the most lovely, generous, welcoming people I know.

To all of the real life Magdalene sisters who I was reunited with during the writing of this book, in particular, but not limited to, Meggan Watterson and Madeline Giles. Your presence unlocked seeds planted long ago.

To my first wise woman Angela Wood, whose chance meeting all those years ago initiated my spiritual path. I look forward to seeing how our relationship continues now you are in a different realm.

To the SSS (Amy Kiberd, Hollie Holden, and Lisa Lister). I am so glad we decided to meet and do all of the rituals together at this time. Your friendship is rejuvenating, and our circle such a refreshing and longed-for holding in my life.

To my mentor Sonia Choquette, for teaching me how to be a teacher, let go of old identities, and lead from the feminine.

To Sheila Dickson and Amy Firth for your friendship through the years.

To the team at Hay House UK (Michelle Pilley, Jo Burgess, Diane Hill, Amy Kiberd, Ruth Tewkesbury, Julie Oughton, Leanne Siu Anastasi, Tom Cole, Alexandra Gruebler, George Lizos, Rachel Dodson, Polina Norina and Sandy Draper), thank you for giving my voice a home, honoring my perfectionist tendencies, and giving me so many opportunities to share my work with the world.

To the team at Hay House Australia (in particular Leon Nacson and Rosie Barry), thank you for supporting my work back home. It is a delight to work with you.

To the team at Hay House USA (particularly Reid Tracy and Kate Riley), thank you for giving my work wings.

To my VA's Michelle Hebbard and Lynsey Cowan for your grounded support and for running the business like clockwork.

To the Magdalenes, Council of Light, guides and Mother Earth, thank you for the endless whispers and using me as a vessel for this message and work.

To the dolphins and whales of Tenerife (and to Winny and Kees Van de Velden, and Hollie and Robert Holden), thank you for reminding me that heaven is a place on Earth.

To Ahlea Khadro, for helping me to embrace my humanness.

To Kyle Gray, for being my Hay House buddy – it's awesome to be doing this work together again.

To the divine masculine in my life who worship the feminine and her sacred work.

Finally to you, my dear reader. It is you I am most grateful for. Thank you for hearing the call. May you always hear the sacred chant beckoning you to Rise Sister Rise.

Love,

Rebecca

ABOUT THE AUTHOR

Jamie Beadon

Rebecca Campbell is a best-selling author, spiritual teacher, grounded spiritual mentor, and devotional soulful guide.

Bestselling author of *Light Is the New Black*, Rebecca has guided thousands of people all over the world to listen to and courageously answer the unique callings of their soul, and create a life that is completely aligned to them. Co-creator of The Spirited Project, Rebecca teaches internationally, helping people to connect with their intuition, birth the creations rising in them, and light up the world with their presence – to serve the world by being themselves.

Renowned for feminine leadership, devotion, and spiritual service, Rebecca has been awarded 'Best Emerging Voice' by *Kindred Spirit*, 'Promising New Talent' by the Mind Body Spirit Festival, and 'Top 100 Women of Spirit' by the Brahama Kumaris. She has featured in publications such as *Elle*, *Red* magazine, *Cosmopolitan*, *The Sunday Times Style* magazine, and *Psychologies*, and on mindbodygreen.com.

Prior to writing books, Rebecca forged a successful career as an award-winning advertising creative director where she helped some of the world's biggest brands find their authentic voice.

Originally from the sunny shores of Sydney, Rebecca now lives in London with her husband and puppy Shakti, but you can find her down under most summers getting her salt water and sunshine fix.

 rebeccathoughts   @rebeccathoughts

www.rebeccacampbell.me

We hope you enjoyed this Hay House book. If you'd like to receive our online catalog featuring additional information on Hay House books and products, or if you'd like to find out more about the Hay Foundation, please contact:

Hay House, Inc., P.O. Box 5100, Carlsbad, CA 92018-5100
(760) 431-7695 or (800) 654-5126
(760) 431-6948 (fax) or (800) 650-5115 (fax)
www.hayhouse.com® • www.hayfoundation.org

***

Published and distributed in Australia by: Hay House Australia Pty. Ltd.,
18/36 Ralph St., Alexandria NSW 2015
Phone: 612-9669-4299 • *Fax:* 612-9669-4144 • www.hayhouse.com.au

Published and distributed in the United Kingdom by: Hay House UK, Ltd.,
Astley House, 33 Notting Hill Gate, London W11 3JQ
Phone: 44-20-3675-2450 • *Fax:* 44-20-3675-2451 • www.hayhouse.co.uk

Published and distributed in the Republic of South Africa by:
Hay House SA (Pty), Ltd., P.O. Box 990, Witkoppen 2068
info@hayhouse.co.za • www.hayhouse.co.za

Published in India by: Hay House Publishers India,
Muskaan Complex, Plot No. 3, B-2, Vasant Kunj, New Delhi 110 070 •
Phone: 91-11-4176-1620 • *Fax:* 91-11-4176-1630 • www.hayhouse.co.in

Distributed in Canada by: Raincoast Books,
2440 Viking Way, Richmond, B.C. V6V 1N2 •
Phone: 1-800-663-5714 • *Fax:* 1-800-565-3770 • www.raincoast.com

***

Take Your Soul on a Vacation

Visit www.HealYourLife.com® to regroup,
recharge, and reconnect with your own magnificence.
Featuring blogs, mind-body-spirit news, and
life-changing wisdom from Louise Hay and friends.

Visit www.HealYourLife.com today!